GRANDPA'S WALK WITH THE LORD

A Life Full of Testimonies

of the

Lord's Involvement

Nov-'19

To my dear friend, Deb ~ may the Lord continue to bless and keep you close

Dean

DEAN BATES

ISBN 978-1-0980-0260-2 (paperback)
ISBN 978-1-0980-0261-9 (digital)

Christian Faith Publishing, Inc.
832 Park Avenue
Meadville, PA 16335
www.christianfaithpublishing.com

Printed in the United States of America

This book is dedicated to each of our grandchildren, that they may realize the valuable heritage that they are privileged to inherit, and learn to actively seek their own walk with the Lord.

This book is also in recognition of the power of the Holy Spirit in my life—a newly discovered understanding that where I refer to the "Lord" in this book, it is truly the living Holy Spirit that has been my guardian, inspiration, and friend, orchestrating all these events in my life.

May the words of my mouth [the words
in this book] and the meditations of
my heart be pleasing in your sight, O
Lord my Rock and my redeemer.
—Psalm 19:14

Contents

Preface

This book is *not* intended to be all about me and what I have accomplished in life. Instead, it is a testimony to the faithfulness of the Lord through the years and generations of the Bates families, and my growth as one of his very own committed sons.

I have always wanted to do the right thing and be an active participant in church activities. I made my way through the minefields of life, just as anyone else would for the first five decades of my life. I come now with no great academic credentials, no outstanding work accomplishments, and I never read the Bible until God revealed himself clearly to me following my rededication to him at age fifty-five. The only personal pride that I have is that I now recognized the part that the Lord has played faithfully throughout my life, and I have to walk with him 24-7.

I believe that the testimonies of his faithfulness are powerful tools that he uses in reaching others, to help them become committed believers in Jesus Christ. It is therefore my desire to be used by him to be inspired to tell my story in a way that brings glory to him, and advances his kingdom.

The focus of this book is to tell my story to my grandchildren so that they may appreciate where their ancestors have come from spiritually. My prayer is that they, and anyone else that reads this book, be inspired and aware of the presence of the Holy Spirit in their life as well. For my family, I appeal to them to carry out the Christian heritage that they are blessed to have inherited.

If you want to enhance the reading of this book, take time to look up each song referenced on the Internet and dwell on the words.

Take this book reading seriously and relate it to your struggles in life, and I can assure you that you might never be the same.

The ultimate purpose is as stated in the book of Colossians:

> That others may be encouraged in heart and united In love, so that we all have the full riches of complete understanding, in order that we may know the mystery of God, namely Christ, in whom are hidden all treasurers of wisdom and knowledge. (Col. 2:2–3, NIV)

Chapter 1

HERITAGE

Although the Bates family has been traced back to the year 1415 in England, the earliest evidence of our Christian commitment to Christ is with two of the members of the Pilgrims on the Mayflower, John Alden and Prescilla Mullins. They arrived in November of 1620, and before setting foot in the new land, they helped form the Mayflower Compact. This Compact, signed by forty-one male members of the Plymouth Colony including John Alden, was a commitment to forming a Christian-based self-government, stating in summary:

> In the name of and the glory of God, and advancement of the Christian faith, we who's names are underwritten, pledge in the presence of God and one another, to plant the first Christian colony in America.

Although half of this colony did not survive the first harsh winter, John Alden and Prescilla Mullins did, and were ultimately married in about 1623. John became prominent in the administration of the colony, and their courtship and marriage became the basis for the classic poem "The Courtship of Myles Standish" by Henry Wadsworth Longfellow.

Their marriage produced ten children. A great-great-grandson became the second president of America, John Adams, whose son, John Quincy Adams, became the sixth president. Up until this time, America did not have a constitution and was subservient to England. John Quincy Adams was one of five men selected to draft the Declaration of Independence.

A granddaughter of John and Prescilla Alden, Hopestill Alden, married Joseph Snow. One of their offspring, Sally Snow, married William Bates in 1764; thus starting the Bates's connection to the Mayflower voyage and to the Alden family. William was a descendent of Edward Bates who had immigrated to America sometime between 1630 and 1640, and was ordained an elder in his church. An elder in those days was commissioned by the Church of England, to establish new churches in America.

In 1803, Ohio became a state in the newly formed United States of America. A great-great-great-great-grandson of Edward, George W. Bates, and his family moved to Ohio in 1842 from New York. It is recorded that they traveled via the recently opened Erie Canal from New York to the west side of Niagara Falls, and then through Lake Erie by ferry boat to Detroit. They eventually settled on land in the Fayette area of northwest Ohio. My great-great-grandfather,

Bates Homestead Farm in Northwest Ohio

George W. Bates bought a farm ten miles east of my hometown that still remains in the family today. My grandfather, Ralph, and his wife, Emma, evidenced their Christian faith by being one of the founding members of what is now the country Christian Church, about three miles from their home, and were active lifetime mem-

bers. This church is still an active parish today, and it has been maintained beautifully.

Country Christian Church

Ralph and Emma had four children: my father, two twin sisters, and my uncle Walter, all of whom have been active in their respective churches and fully committed to their faith. Walter and his wife, Mary Jane, were lifetime members of the country church, east of the family farm about three miles. Walter was a Sunday school teacher for many years and was the primary one to help maintain and preserve this historic structure. One of my aunts, Leota, married a doctor, Homer Isley. They were very committed Christians and later in their marriage, provided the building materials for starting an American Indian village church in Arizona. They drove a truck from Michigan loaded with these materials, helped build the church for the Navajo Nation, and then donated the truck. My other aunt, Viola, a twin-sister to Leota, was a school teacher in Lower Michigan and a very active participant in the Methodist Church in town. She was well known for her baking, often making beautiful rolls, bread, and as many as seven or eight pies for events in the Church.

My father, Donald, married my mother, Leona Griffin, and had five boys. I was the second oldest, born in 1934. My parents were very dedicated members of the Methodist Church all of their married life, and all of my brothers and myself were very active in our faith. My older brother, Richard, became a Methodist Pastor in Texas in his later years when he retired. My brother, Lyle, is a very active member of an organization that distributes Bibles in hotels and motels in the fast-growing area of South Carolina. My youngest brother, Elwyn, performs Christian carioca singing in nursing homes and care facilities near our hometown in Ohio.

My mother's father, Walter Griffin, was the grandson of a pioneer settler, William Griffin, who brought his wife in 1837 to the northwest Ohio area. They were living in New York and traveled out through the Erie Canal that had recently been completed. He purchased forty acres and then sixty more of virgin land that was part of an extensive area west of Lake Erie called the Black Swamp. To provide temporary shelter when they arrived, it is reported that they turned the wagon over and stayed under it while clearing the property and building a home. This property is still in the Griffin family to this day, located one mile east and one-half mile south of my hometown. In 1838, one of their sons, William Henry, was the first male child born in the Township. Altogether, William had three wives and twenty-seven children, including fourteen stepchildren.

The year after William's arrival the township built their first school, a one-room log cabin. After it was opened, a group of people gathered in the school house to begin the Methodist Episcopal Church, and the Griffin family was active in its foundation. A year later, they built their own church building that was a wood frame structure. In 1878, a new brick church building was completed. Twelve years later, in 1880, this building was destroyed by fire; a conflagration by arsonists that took out fifty structures in town. The current church was completed in 1905 and is an impressive structure with a dome in the sanctuary that is approximately forty feet high. The church has all stain glass windows throughout, including two very large ones in the sanctuary that are approximately fifteen feet high. What an awesome dedication to our Lord, considering the time period, built without the benefit of any power tools or construction technology.

My hometown United Methodist Church

One of two large stain glass windows

When Katie and I were married, Grandpa Griffin wrote a letter, passing on his wisdom, and he was a true gentleman in all respects:

> Success is not merely the accumulation of great wealth and property, but a well-rounded life of peace, happiness and enough of the worldly goods for comfort, with a little uneasiness thrown in from time to time is of benefit as it forces one on to greater efforts and eventually you have gained the objective which everyone should set to accomplish. Value your word as you would your life. Your word is worth more to you many times

than the actual means. When you hear someone remark "He is honest and his word is as good as gold," it is one of the greatest compliments one can have said of him.

The early pioneers lived a life of very hard work, clearing the land of timber with ax, handsaw, and horses. They lived among land that the Indians had their homes. Fire was a constant threat, and our town lost fifty structures including their church. Electricity had not been invented yet. Tractors were yet to come. There were no power tools. Creature comforts were primitive, to say the least. And yet they felt very blessed to be Americans and were faithful in their expressions of gratitude to the Lord by building and attending churches at a time that incomes were extremely low. May we live our lives in honor of our heritage and to be extremely grateful to our Lord for the abundance that we now enjoy.

> Faith of our Fathers! Living still in spite of dan-
> ger, fire
> and sword;
> O how our hearts beat high with joy,
> Whenever we hear that glorious word!
> Faith of our fathers, Holy faith!
> We will be true to thee till death!

> —Fredrick W. Foster

Chapter 2

GROWING UP

The earliest memories of my growing up were in a family of five boys in the small town in Ohio. This village is located in very fertile farmland of northwestern Ohio. It was a very small town of about one thousand people, and we lived within forty miles of my grandparents, two great-grandmothers, and six aunts and uncles. They were all very loving and caring people, always welcoming us into their homes. Our family and all our aunts and uncles' families would gather at Grandpa and Grandma Bates's farm several times each year for a Sunday dinner, making hand-cranked homemade ice cream, the men driving around the countryside talking men-things, shooting rats in the barn and night using a flashlight, and just thoroughly enjoying each other. As a small boy, I would periodically stay with each of them for a weekend in their homes and was very much loved on. As I look back, none of them consumed alcohol; they all lived an honorable life and were not only faithful in church attendance but actively participated in all activities. Their relationships were all loving, with no divorces, to my knowledge, in any of our families. At one time, my father was diagnosed as having very low blood pressure. The doctor suggested that he could take a shot of whiskey every day to help, and my dad's response was, "I would rather die first."

My great-great-grandfather, George W. Griffin, along with my grandpa Walter Griffin were founding fathers of the Methodist Church and were all lifetime members. Walter was an insurance agent with an office downtown and owned a very nice home about three blocks from our home. He was a real gentleman and highly respected in the community. I loved going to his home on Sunday afternoon, to play anagrams and caroms—games long ago forgotten about.

Our house was moved from the Griffin homestead east of town. It was originally a two-story house, and then a single-story addition was added for our family. We moved in within one year of my birth, in 1935, and it remains in the family to this day. It was not uncommon in those days, to move houses and even barns. There were no trucks or tractors at the time, and logs were used to roll them along, pulled by horses.

When my mother was a small child, she was given a book about Jesus by her aunt. This book was handmade, consisting of cloth pages with illustrations and stories about Jesus sewn on the pages. The pages were then sewn together, creating a binding. In reflecting on the times, there were no children's books published and available for purchase. Also, there were no published textbooks for school, and the Bible was used to teach reading, writing, and our spiritual heritage. The Christian message was taught to everyone!

I was born in the middle of the Great Depression, in 1934. Our property included a two-story barn and an extensive backyard for a large, wonderful garden. We raised chickens for meat and eggs in the barn, and had a goat for milk for me, as I was allergic to cow's milk. We always had plenty to eat, even for five growing boys, and we rarely purchased food.

The goat was a favorite of us kids. We would occasionally hitch the goat to a little red wagon and participate in the local annual harvest festival in town. Our school house consisted of one nice brick building for all twelve grades (no kindergarten in those days), and we had to walk about three-fourth miles across town to get there. We always were expected to walk to and from school in all kinds of weather. When I started first grade, my parents bought me a bright yellow raincoat and rain hat. The first time that I wore them, my friend from across the street, Larry, walked home from school with me. We ended up going to the barn to say hello to the goat. We got to talking about how goats are reported to eat anything. I said that surely Jack, the goat, would not be interested in my rain hat, as it was made of rubber. I offered it to him, he smelled it, and he suddenly grabbed it out of my hand and digested the whole thing on the spot. When I told my parents, they thought it was funny and did not discipline me, but I never got another hat.

During these younger years, we always went to Sunday school and church. Each year that we faithfully attended Sunday school without fail, we were awarded a small wreath pin that I proudly wore on the lapel of my suit jacket. We always wore a suit, white shirt, and tie, along with dress shoes. In subsequent years, we were awarded an attachment below the wreath for faithful Sunday school attendance without a miss, and I ended up with many of them. I really enjoyed all of my church experiences. During the summer, I would attend the week-long vacation Bible school (VBS) at the Methodist Church. After that ended, I would go to the local Nazarene Church to attend their VBS, as it was something to do, and I was attracted to their loving environment. During this time we were taught many things, but we were also expected to memorize all names of the books of the Bible, New and Old Testament. To this day, I can still rattle off most of the names in sequence, but age is beginning to take its toll. When I became old enough (about ten) I attended a three-day church camp located about one hundred miles away on a lake in Ohio. This was a big deal, as it was the first time away from the family. A few years later, I attended a one-week church camp at on Lake Erie. This was a thrill and a really big event in my life. It was at this camp, at the Saturday night service, that I asked Jesus into my heart and my life. Unfortunately, from that point on for the next forty years of faithful church attendance, I never came to realize that this acceptance meant that Jesus knew me and he had a plan for my life if I were to just seek it. It took me until age fifty-five to come to understand this, but in the meantime he faithfully helped me to have confidence and courage to venture out, and to keep me safe. I will address these experiences later.

Using bad language in our home was a definite no-no. The punishment, even if we used questionable language, was two tablespoons of a digestion that was a very chalky substance and left a coating on your tongue. Obviously, I was caught a few times and as a result I have always had an aversion to cottage cheese. I do remember one time, on a Sunday evening while my parents were having a Bible study group in their home, I must have said something that was not appropriate as I got the "treatment." Again, as a cadet in the academy where in the military using foul words is part of everyday language, I came out with an inappropriate word in front of my parents. Nothing was said, but the silence was convicting. What a lesson, Lord, that I have not forgotten after all of these years!

When I was about four years old, I wanted us to have a dog. We found a pup on a farm near home, and she was part Pekinese and part Pomeranian. She was a very gentle dog that we named Boots, as she was mostly black with white feet. Of us five boys, my next youngest brother was Neil, three years junior to me. Soon after he was able to walk he wandered away from home without any of us being aware. Mom got a call from a friend nearby, informing her that Neil and Boots were setting on the curb along Highway 20, a main highway through town. The friend told Mom that she saw Boots grab Neil's diaper and set him down on the curb as he was about to walk onto the highway. Thank you, Lord, for our little dog Boots to save Neil from harm.

In the third grade, I wanted to learn to play the drums. My parents felt that it would be best to start by learning the basics of music on the piano, and after a year or so, I could proceed with the drums. My Grandma Griffin encouraged me to take piano lessons and agreed to pay for them. She and Grandpa were avid supporters of music in the town. In 1882 they, along with a brother, George Griffin, had been major contributors in establishing the town's Normal Music and Business College. This college eventually was moved and has now become a state university. Grandpa and Grandma were prominent in supporting the town's music program in high school, and in 1939 the school won the National Orchestra Contest award, presented in Ottawa, Kansas.

100th Birthday Monday

Grandma Griffin

Unfortunately, the only piano teacher in this small town would only teach playing classical music, not popular music. Although the popular music of the '40s was what I wanted to learn, I stuck with the lessons through high school. I never felt that I was good at it and did not enjoy playing for others. However, I learned to sight read very well and bought whatever popular sheet music that I could find, to enjoy playing popular music. What I was playing always seemed so structured, and if I did not memorize the music I could not play it on my own. I wanted to learn to play by "ear," but never did until I was seventy years old. I will address this subject later in this book.

I enjoyed music and joined the church choir as a young teen. I only played the drums for a year and then I took up the tenor saxophone. I continued with the saxophone through high school and beyond. The local Fulton County school system sponsored a band and chorus concert each year, and I participated in both for several years. During high school, four of us classmates and I formed a saxophone quartet. We would play at a few events such as the Women's

Club or any other group that we could get excused from school to perform. For three years, our quartet participated in the Ohio State musical competition, and won first place each time. After high school, I was invited to join a dance band that played at a nearby social lodge once a month. This was really enjoyable as we played the big band music of the '40s.

At age twelve, I started delivering the *Toledo Blade* newspaper with weekday delivery. From that point on, I was able to earn enough money to buy my own clothes and had my own spending money. I was, thereby, able to purchase a new Schwinn bicycle, the latest type of camera, a Polaroid, and a used motor attachment for my bicycle for twenty-five dollars. It needed an overhaul that I figured out without a manual of any sorts. After installing it on my bicycle, I got what I thought was gasoline that I found in the barn. When I tried to start the motor, it refused to run. Afterward, I found out from my dad that the gas can contained kerosene instead of gas—another lesson learned. With fresh gas, it ran perfectly for the next few years. My friend, Robin, bought a new motorbike, and we had so much fun driving together over the nearby countryside.

The experience that I got from delivering newspapers I learned valuable lessons about the need to satisfy my customers, accounting for payments, and persistence in dealing with all types of people and weather. One of my customers was a nice, elderly lady who gave me a beautiful, very small New Testament Bible with wood front and back covers. These covers were made from an olive tree from the Holy Land. How regrettable that I did not learn the background of this Bible, as I was given it about four years after the country of Israel was reestablished in 1948. I still have this Bible and cherish it to this today.

My paper route consisted of a wide assortment of people, consisting of up to fifty-five customers. I made three cents per paper—big money for a teenager in those days. My customers included a bakery where I would purchase a jelly donut every day (for three cents). Next door was a tavern where I would take a big breath, walk fast into the bar, lay the paper down, and walk out fast before I caught my next breath. The Saturday collection, however, was something else. On

Saturdays, I would take time to chat with my customers, including a lady that collected porcelain dolls, the owner of a blacksmith shop, the local druggist, the pastor of our church, and a farmer half a mile out of town where I ended up mowing his big yard by hand, pushing a mower with no motor.

When I was thirteen my older brother Dick, who was three years older, decided to purchase a shotgun and to take up hunting. He had been out rabbit hunting one Saturday and came home to skin the rabbits and clean the double-barrel shotgun. He used a card table to clean the gun on, and we were setting opposite each other in the kitchen. After cleaning it, he opened the chamber, inserted a shell, and closed it just to check out the mechanism. For some reason, when he closed the chamber, the gun suddenly fired. Fortunately, the gun was pointed to the side of us, and we just stared at each other in complete shock. Our mother was upstairs, ran down and found us "frozen" in place, but okay. The gun shot a large hole in the sink cabinet, went through the sink, and out the back side of the house. Needless to say, my brother never shot the weapon again, sold it, and that ended his interest in hunting. Thank you, Lord, for saving us from harm.

In 1878, George Griffin and a friend purchased the *Fayette Record* local newspaper and changed the name to Lewis and Griffin Record. In 1901, this newspaper was purchased by Charles Yost, and it was renamed the *Fayette Review.* In the 1940s it reverted to Herb, a friend of our family, who also was the editor. For the last two years of high school, I worked for this newspaper, helping to publish it weekly. There were only the two of us to produce this four-page, full-size newspaper that was mailed out on Friday morning to the subscribers. This newspaper covered local events, high school activities, deaths, births, marriages, and out-of-state visitors as well as advertisements. A linotype machine was used to set the main text, and the headings were added manually from a large set of drawers of individual letters (fonts) and a variety of types and sizes. The linotype machine was like a typewriter and consisted of lead ingots that were melted in the machine. The typesetting part of the machine allowed the melted lead to form on the type face, cool and ejected into a tray as individual "lines of type." Herb operated the machine but I helped put this into a large metal frame where the page layouts occurred, headings and advertisements were added, and then clamped into two full-size pages at a time. These frames were then assembled on the printing table, an ink roller would run over the type, and then a very large roller with individual sheets of paper were pressed over the type two pages at a time. This paper had to be manually fed into the top of this device, and that was one of my jobs. After all four pages were printed, a separate folding machine would be used to form a deliverable newspaper. On Saturday morning, my job was to melt the lines of type in a heater, skim off the residue, and form the ingots that would be used in the linotype machine. This was a great experience, and when I graduated from high school I expected to make publishing newspapers a career. As the fate on most newspapers today, they have gone out of business.

The high school graduation ceremony for our class was held in our Methodist Church. This was because a new gymnasium was under construction, and our church was the next largest gathering place in town. This is the only time in history that graduation was ever held outside of the school—and in a church. As a total surprise to me, at this ceremony I was given an award, a book titled *I Dare You*. The award was presented, by vote of the teachers, to the graduating student reflecting the best potential for success in life. I was floored, as I never felt that I was anything special. This book offers encouragement and advice to individuals that want to achieve their greatest potential in life. This boosted my confidence and determination to do my very best in the future. The book is still in print today, and still stresses the importance of faith and trust in the future.

Herb was also a private pilot and encouraged me to join the local Civil Air Patrol (CAP). This was a county-wide organization of pilots, and the local chapter met once a month, with pilots that owned their own airplanes. As a cadet, this gave me an opportunity to fly, and our primary mission was to perform search and rescue missions for downed aircraft. A Dawn Patrol group, usually consisting of two or three airplanes, would often take off at the crack of dawn and fly over this beautiful country of Northwestern Ohio. Ten of us cadets joined together, collected thirty-five each, and bought a very basic trainer with which we could take flying lessons. I took a total of six lessons and was about to "solo" when other events took over my life. During one of these lessons while practicing power-off stalls, the throttle stuck at idle when I went to recover. The instructor assured me that it was no big problem, just pick out a field to land in. We did and landed safely; fortunately, in a recently harvested wheat field, thank you, Lord! The instructor got out, freed-up the throttle, got in, and took off without damage to the airplane or to the farmer's field. Whee! Thank you, Lord! About this time, the Ohio CAP offered me a one-week all-expenses paid trip as an exchange cadet to Europe that I had to decline as I was entering West Point.

In the spring of 1951, when I was a junior in high school, I was asked by a local farmer to work for him in the spring and summer. This farmer, Cal, was a young Ohio State graduate who was newly married and was a friend of our family and member of the Methodist Church. The year after he had graduated from high school, he had gone to the Naval Academy for a four-year education. While at the academy, however, WWII was in progress and he wanted to participate, so he resigned from the academy and accepted a commission in the Naval Air Corps. Upon graduation from pilot training, he was assigned to a multi-engine airplane, an amphibious PBY, and was on his way to the Pacific when the war ended. He then came home, entered Ohio State University, and graduated with a degree in agriculture. He had recently come back to the farm to take over the family operation and needed help. I started working in the spring part-time, and at the end of the school year, I went out to work full time for the summer. Unbeknownst to me Cal's wife, Barb, sent an invitation to her sister, Katie, to visit the farm and meet this "handsome farmhand." Katie lived about two hours away, in Ann Arbor, Michigan. The invitation was written on two-penny postcards, as there was too much to say for one. Katie has kept these postcards in her box of memories ever since. When she came to the farm to visit, she came out to meet me in the adjoining field where I was feeding the pigs. I took her for a ride on the tractor, and we've been lovers ever since. She came out wearing one of her brother's white shirt with the tails tied together—an unusual sight to behold on the farm. From that time on for the next six years, we never lived near each other except for holidays and special occasions, and we kept writing letters the entire time. Katie kept all of my letters still stored in my attic today.

My dear Katie Clark

At the time I met Katie, I had a bad case of acne and considered that no girl would want to date me, so I hadn't dated at all throughout high school. This had given me a somewhat inferiority complex, so I didn't feel good about myself. What especially impressed me about Katie was that she didn't seem to care about my complexion problem and liked me anyway. Wow, what a special lady! It turned out that she had lost her father to a heart attack one year earlier, her family was leaving their home and going separate ways, and she needed a friend. Well, she sure found one in me. After writing letters for the next six years and only occasionally seeing each other, we were finally married in the big chapel on the hill at West Point. But I'm getting ahead of myself...Lord, I will forever be grateful for you arranging for Katie to be my wife and loving partner!

While working on the farm, Cal encouraged me to take a special Civil Service examination being offered the following Saturday at the county seat in Wauseon, Ohio. This examination was to be used as the basis for the local representative to congress, to make his appointments to the academies. There were only three of us that took the examination, and I was offered a first-alternate appointment to the Naval Academy, and a principle appointment to West Point. I didn't want to risk losing out on such an opportunity of a free four-year college education, so I accepted the West Point appointment. I would still have to pass the entrance exams that were to be given the following January. This appointment came about in early September for entrance the following June and would lead to a bachelor's degree in engineering. I knew, without a shadow of a doubt, that I was very deficient in my academic skills. I was not expecting to go to college as I had too much fun with extracurricular activities in high school, so I immediately enrolled in the local community college, taking all of the same courses that I would have the first year at West Point. This college was thirty miles away. As "luck" would have it, we had a neighbor two blocks from home that drove by our house every morning and worked in the area of the college. He drove there every day and went right by the college. This was clearly a God-created help to fill my transportation needs and qualify me for entrance to the academy. What a blessing, Lord, and I take this was a confirmation that this is your plan for me!

My philosophy during high school was that developing social skills was equally as important as academic skills. For that reason, I was involved in everything I was inspired to do in that regard. In addition to my musical activities, this included helping organize a chess club, participating in the junior and senior class plays, joining with the town adults to put on a minstrel show, organizing a basketball pep band that played at ball games, and participating on the high school track team. I also practiced with the church organist, Geneva, and played piano/organ duets with her. Unfortunately, this enjoyable lifestyle resulted in my pride of never having taken a book home to study the entire time in high school. For me it was okay as long as I received passing grades (no D's or F's) and was enjoying myself. I had never considered going to college, as the economy of the times was very tough following the end of WWII and none of my immediate family had graduated with a four-year college degree. Some of my relatives had nursing and teaching degrees, but couldn't afford the costs of going to college, and I was looking forward to a career in newspaper publishing.

When at the local college, I joined the student choir. This was a forty-nine-voice a cappella choir and directed by a very prominent musician. It turned out that he had been a speech writer for General Eisenhower during WWII. During the 1952 presidential election, General Eisenhower was elected president of the United States, and our choir was invited to sing during the president's inaugural ceremony on the steps of the Capitol. That we did in February, and the choir sang the president's favorite hymn, "Lead Kindly Light." What a thrill. Thank you, Lord!

My participation in President Eisenhower's first inauguration

General Eisenhower was the commander in chief of the Allied forces in Europe for the Normandy Invasion and for defeating Nazi Germany, ending WWII. This was a time in which the Cold War was developing, when both Russia and the U.S. had nuclear weapons, and the threat of war seemed emanate. In addition to the Cold War, he was elected to lead us while we were facing the Korean War, a fragile economy, and a very uncertain future for the country. Thus, this hymn had become so meaningful to him through these conflicts that he had experienced in his leadership role as a military commander:

> Lead, kindly Light, amid the encircling gloom,
> Lead thou me on!
> The night is dark, and I am far from home;
> Lead thou me on!
> Keep thou my feet, I do not ask to see
> The distant scene, one step enough for me.

—John Henry Newman

At the end of the college school year, my English teacher predicted that I would never get through West Point with the English skills that I had. A similar comment was made by my German teacher, as I found these courses very challenging. How prophetic these comments turned out, as they were the major challenges that I experienced later at the academy. Unbeknownst to me, however, by taking these courses at the community college, they would exempt me from having to take the equivalent entrance exams in January for admission to West Point. Therefore, when I went for the entrance exams, I only had to pass a social studies exam and the physical requirements, both of which I passed easily. These entrance exams were administered at an Army base just north of Chicago. I had to travel there via rail in a snowstorm, from Ohio to Chicago, and then another train to the Army post north of the city. This was quite an experience for a kid from the farm country of Ohio, whose family had never traveled by train. Although I passed these entrance requirements easily, I have always considered that I was ushered into the academy by the grace of God, despite my deficiencies.

In order to get to West Point when entering in early June, I had to take a train from to Albany, NY, and then on to New York City. I then had to take a taxi to a train station in New Jersey where I caught a train to West Point on the West Shore Railroad along the Hudson River. An abrupt change was about to begin that would change my life forever. Looking back at it, I realize that I got there not of my own intentions and planning, but a willingness to accept the opportunities and challenges that the Lord offered me in order to follow his plan for my life, and not necessarily mine.

> Jesus calls us; o'er the tumult
> Of our life's wild, restless sea;
> Day by day, His sweet voice soundeth,
> Saying, "Christian, follow Me!"
>
> Jesus calls us! By Thy mercies,
> Savior, may we hear Thy call,
> Give our hearts to Thine obedience,
> Serve and love Thee best of all.
>
> —Cecil F. Alexander

I have had a firm belief, all along, that I did not have to fear the future. I have always had an adventurous spirit, with confidence that whatever I got myself into, the Lord would get me out. My history has shown that my upbringing gave me a solid basis of faith and confidence that I need not fear anything, with hard work and integrity guiding my efforts. I have enjoyed being an optimist and have always tried to:

> Look for the silver lining,
> Whenever a cloud appears in the blue.
> Remember somewhere the sun is shining,
> And so the right thing to do is make it shine for
>   you.

A heart full of joy and gladness
Will always banish sadness and strife,
So always look for the silver lining
And try to find the sunny side of life.

Lyrics by B. G. DeSylva
Sung by Judy Garland

(I suggest you Google "Look for the Silver
Lining" sung by Aretha Franklin)

Chapter 3

WEST POINT

Upon arrival at West Point, I was immediately introduced to the most abrupt change in life's circumstances that I could ever have imagined. Every freedom was taken away, with only the choice to obey or go home. My hair was cut off completely, we marched everywhere, we had to eat setting at attention while upper classmen queried us, and we couldn't even go to the restroom without escort and permission. We couldn't talk to each other except in our rooms, we had to memorize many things and recite them upon demand, and the calisthenics and athletic demands were considerable. Every night before going to bed, we were marched to the showers, given two minutes for a shower after which we had to dry off, salute, and report, "Sir, I have showered and dried, shaved (in the morning), and have had a bowel movement in the last twenty-four hours (if you did; if not, when was the last time?)."

During the next year, we were slowly given back some of our freedoms, one at a time. For the entire time, however, we ate at attention with our eyes on our plate, spoke only when spoken to, and had to serve the upper classmen with their desires for seconds, coffee, tea, desert, etc. A *New York Times* newspaper was delivered to our rooms each day (except weekends), and we were expected to be current on national and international events, movies and musical events, sports, as well as the calendar of local events at the academy for the coming week, and we were queried on such knowledge.

We were not marched to our classes but walked at attention without talking to other classmates, saluting all officers. We were expected to be in the classroom standing at our desk, at attention, at the appointed time when the bell rang. If we were one second late, it was as bad as one hour late. Our course assignments were to be self-taught, with help from our classmates if possible. At the start of the class, the instructor would ask if there were any questions, that must be specific and not a general question such as "I don't understand…" This was only for a few minutes before the instructor would announce "Take Boards." We then went to the blackboards and given questions to be answered. These answers were then graded by the instructor after class was over and we had left. We were graded each day in every class, and the results were posted at the end of each week, included running averages. We always knew exactly where we stood grade-wise, on a scale of 3.0 maximum, with 2.0 cutoff as being deficient.

We were not able to leave the post for the first year, except for the Army/Navy football game in Philadelphia. For that game, we were all transported by train, and were gone only for that one day, with freedom after the game until having to meet at the train at eleven o'clock, for a late-night trip back to the academy.

At Christmastime, my parents and four brothers drove out to be with me during the holidays. During these holidays we first-year cadets, plebes, were at "at ease" and able to relax without upper class-men. When my family arrived, they discovered, however, that I was "assigned to quarters" until I was evaluated in the Portuguese language course that I was taking. My average had dropped slightly below 2.0 and, therefore, I was subject to being "washed out" (dismissed) if I did not pass this special evaluation. I did pass after the two-day evaluation consisting of writing and an oral quizzing in front of a panel of officers. I was then allowed to join my family for a very memorable time during the holidays. My family could eat dinners in the mess hall with us plebes, and the meals were wonderful; especially for our family that was not used to shrimp, steak, and other special treats. My brother, Richard, was married and could not come. However, Katie did come with my family, and that was so special for us both.

In February of the first year, I was so discouraged with my struggles that I seriously wanted to quit and go home. Somehow, my aunt Leota and uncle Homer Isley found out my state of depression and flew out from Michigan to JFK and drove up to visit me one weekend. During our conversations, they explained that when they were married, in the early years of WWII, Leota was a nurse working with a doctor in a small town in Lower Michigan, while Homer was attending medical school in Louisville, Kentucky. They had little money, so Leota worked with Doctor Blanchard, to begin the first hospital in Morenci, and send money to Homer to pay for his schooling and his expenses. Money was so tight that she would buy rolls of cloth and cut out and make the sheets and pillow cases for the hospital. They did not live together as a married couple for the two years that Homer had left to complete medical school and became a doctor. What a struggle as newlyweds, but the results were worth overcoming the difficulties. The time that we had together, during this visit, was enough to inspire me to continue pressing on and not give up! What they had experienced in their early years of marriage was extremely impressive and helped put my struggles in perspective.

Regarding my relationship with Katie, she faithfully wrote me two letters each week during the entire four years. In turn, I would write her once each week, primarily to pour out my challenges and frustrations, as she was a great sounding board. As it turned out, Katie has kept every one of my letters, and they are still stored in the attic of our home. I have not had courage enough yet to read any of them, as it would remind me of such a very bleak time in my life. My second summer, Katie accepted a position as a counselor at a youth camp in the Catskill Mountains about thirty miles from West Point. She did not have a car but thought that somehow there would be transportation to the academy so that we could see each other sometime while she was so close. As it turned out, there was no way to get to West Point the entire summer until the camp closed, and then she somehow worked her way over to see me for a weekend, before returning to college in Michigan. Bummer!

In the spring of my third year, we were allowed to leave the academy during the week of Easter, from Wednesday to Sunday night at six o'clock in the evening. My friend and fellow classmate, Don, from Wyandotte near Detroit, flew out with me to Detroit, for time with our families and our future wives. Katie and Don's girlfriend, Kay, were roommates in college. On the way back to the academy on our early Sunday morning flight to JFK in New York, we both fell asleep as we had stayed up most of the previous nights. When we were awakened by a flight attendant, she informed us that they were parked at the airport in Philadelphia, as there was a snowstorm at JFK, and they had to be diverted. So…how do we now get to West Point?

We managed to make our way from Philadelphia to New York City via bus, arriving at the city bus terminal late that afternoon. Because of the storm, all connecting bus schedules to the academy were cancelled. We decided to try to get to the West Side Railroad in New Jersey where there was train service to the academy. From the New York City bus station, we tried to take a taxi to the train station but, because of the heavy snowstorm, no one would take us. We then took a subway to the vicinity of the George Washington Bridge, and from there we were going to hitch a ride across the bridge to the train station. A man came by in a Cadillac, and he knew exactly where the train terminal was and drove us there. When we arrived he pointed out that the building, which we couldn't see because of the snowstorm, was just up the walkway over the hill. By now, it was dark but we headed up the hill as he drove away. When we got to the terminal, we discovered that it was locked and would not open until just before the next train would come, that would be about three hours later. We found ourselves locked out, in our spring cadet uniforms, and without any winter overcoats or gloves. We needed to go somewhere warm for the three hours, so we went back to the street. We couldn't see a house light because of the snow that was coming down, and there were no houses in the immediate area.

While we were standing there bewildered, a pickup truck stopped and offered us a ride to his home nearby. It turned out that he was a Good Samaritan that was cruising around helping to pull people out of the snow, who needed help. (Thank you, Lord!) He lived about a mile away and, when we pulled into his driveway, the truck stopped by itself, and all electrical power was lost including the headlights. It would not start, so he said to come into the house and stay until it was time to walk back to the terminal. He and his wife fed us, and when it was time, he got out a child's sled on which we put our luggage, and we all walked back to the train station. The train did arrive soon after, about 10:30 p.m., and we arrived at the academy soon after midnight, over six hours late. At seven o'clock the next morning, we were required to report to the officer in charge of our company to explain why we were late. There were dozens of other cadets that were also late, as so many of them lived in the East and road traffic turned out to be a disaster. As a result of the story that we told, the officer reported that Don and I had sufficiently planned ahead, but were caught in circumstances that we could not have anticipated, but kept trying to get to the academy as soon as possible. Our story was so bizarre that we were excused from any repercussions. It turned out that we were the only cadets, of the dozens that were late, that avoided punishment. Thank you, Lord, for no reprimands.

In June, a few months later, I became a first classmen (senior), and I was assigned the rank of private. Our first summer assignment was a trip to Wright-Patterson Air Force Base at Dayton, Ohio. This was about a four-hour drive for Katie and Kay, to visit us from Michigan, and they came with two other girls for "blind dates." We could see them Saturday afternoon and evening but had to be back to our quarters at 11:00 p.m. We all went to the city for the evening, with an understanding that we would meet at the car at ten o'clock, giving us plenty of time to get back to the base without being late. When the time came to meet, one couple did not show up for twenty-five minutes, and the amount of time left was very questionable as to whether we could make it on time. I decided that I would have to drive instead of Katie to meet the reporting time. Driving was not permitted by the academy on the base. I drove somewhat risky, even on the base, and arrived at the barracks with less than five minutes to spare. As I got out of the car, the officer in charge was standing there and I was, obviously, in trouble. I lost my rank and had other disciplinary action.

During my last year, Katie had graduated from Ypsilanti State Teachers College in Michigan and was able to get a job in Somerville, NJ, so as to be near me at West Point for my last year. She had majored in teaching special-education children, but her job was in elementary school as a regular teacher. Although we have many good memories of this year, unfortunately my struggles were compounded through more circumstances that were not directly of my making. My rank had been taken away, as I previously explained, and I spent some amount of time "confined to quarters" from even more difficulties that I experienced.

Although as cadets we were introduced to many sports, the one that I enjoyed the most was handball. This was a club, and they had a competitive arrangement where we played other members and were ranked on the "Handball Ladder." When a trip came up, the top ten cadets on the ladder were selected for the trip to play other teams. A trip to NYC came up in the winter to play the New York Athletic Club, members of who were adults from NYC. I qualified, and we went down by bus on Saturday morning. This was about a two-hour drive, and we were given box lunches to eat en route. We played in the afternoon soon after arrival. The club consisted of mid- and older age seniors that, obviously, had been playing handball for many years. We young cadets, with our energy and enthusiasm, could not begin to keep up with their experience and accuracy. They could place the ball so well that, if they had to hustle for it, they didn't need it, so let us occasionally score a point or two. They really enjoyed beating us young cadets and afterward, their club rewarded us with a very nice, semi-formal dinner. They took us to a restaurant that specialized in lobster. Knowing that we cadets probably had never eaten lobster, they introduced us to how to get all the good stuff out, even from the claws.

Front Row (left to right): Maliska, T. P.; Ellington, J. D.; Monaco, N.; Solberg, A. M.
Second Row (left to right): Bates, D. E.; DeSola, J. R.; Rogers, C. C.; Murtland, R. C.; Roth, M. F.; Halloway, K. E.; Lt. Col. A. N. Thompson (Officer-in-Charge).

Handball Club

C-2, FIRST CLASS: (left to right)
1st Row—Rose, BT; Delaney, D; Barrett, A; Carroll, W; Magadieu, W; As
2nd Row—Markham, R; Rosenberg, TM; Hindman, C; Tonda, RD. *3rd Row*—Hal
Pocock, JA; Adams, JE; Vickers, JH; Newman, EM; Hanford, JO. *4th Row*—H
Murchison, J; Bates, DE; Dodson, JP. *5th Row*—McConnell, RD; Hicklin, T;
Beckwith, R. *Absent:* Day, HE.

39

As I have mentioned, Katie landed a job teaching in an elementary school in Summerville, NJ, so that she could be near for weekend events. When we were finished with dinner with the New York Athletic Club, she came over to pick me up to stay at the home where she had rented a room. The next day, I was to be back to the Taft Hotel in NYC at four in the afternoon to catch the bus back to the academy. We left Summerville with plenty of time but, as we were approaching the Lincoln Tunnel, all traffic came to a complete stop. There had, apparently, been an accident in the tunnel, and for the next hour or more, we were at a complete standstill with no alternative other than to wait it out. Finally, traffic started moving again, but by the time we got to the Taft Hotel, I was ten minutes late. Unfortunately, I jumped out of the car and Katie drove off before I realized that the bus had already departed, and I had no money for any kind of transportation back to the academy. I knew that the owner of the hotel, a lady who had a special affection for West Point, so I went to the front desk and asked to speak with her. They connected me through, I explained my circumstances, and she sent down enough money for me to get a bus ticket to the academy. Needless to say, I was in trouble upon arrival, with more in-room confinement and "walking the area." Even worse, a few more weekends that I could not see Katie.

In order to help keep the moral up, it was a bit of a sport to try to get away with something. My little claim to fame was that I had my mother send me an electric popcorn popper and some corn. It was, of course, against the rules to cook anything in our rooms. I fashioned, from a wire coat hanger, a way in which I could store the popper in the back corner of the bed, attached to the springs. Unless you knew it was there, it would be unlikely that it would ever be found. On an occasional Saturday night when we couldn't go anywhere, I would make up a batch for us, and then clean and store it before the smell would get out. Of course, the smell would drift around and occasionally the officer in charge would drop by to investigate. This was not a serious offense and the Honor Code did not require us to tell where it was. It was always taken in good humor by the officer, and I never got caught.

One of my good friends and a classmate was Jack Adams. He had been in the Army as a paratrooper in the Korean War and had performed a number of jumps including two combat jumps. He was not one to "sweat the small stuff," and he was not too thrilled to have to put up with "Mickey Mouse" nonsense. During our first Christmas holidays when we had to stay on the post, he had a friend from the outside bring him a couple of beers. One of our classmates happened upon Jack's room, found him with a beer, and felt duty-bound to report him under the Honor Code. Such reporting was not required, but Jack got in serious trouble over it and was restricted to quarters for three months, walking the area with his rifle each Wednesday afternoon for two hours, and Saturday afternoon for three hours, etc. At the end of January, Jack was so glad that the first months' restrictions were over that he tore off January's calendar, lit it on fire, and then tossed it in the trash can. Unfortunately, there was flame enough to catch the can on fire, and he had to take it out into the hall to extinguish it in the sink. With the smoke and commotion, an upper classman caught him and reported the incident, followed by more discipline for Jack. A few weeks later, a classmate arranged to come to Jack's room for some tutoring at a certain time in the evening. Jack thought it would be cute to rig up a glass of water that was placed on the fluorescent light fixture, with a string attached and routed to the door. The intention was that, when the door was opened, the glass of water would tip over on him. Good clean humor! Unfortunately, the officer in charge happened to drop in for a look-see. When he opened the door, it was not opened quite enough for the glass to tip over. As he was leaving, however, he opened the door a bit more and down came the water. So…Jack was in trouble again. We always knew when Jack was reporting to his commanding officer, as he dressed in his best uniform and put on all of his ribbons, which were very impressive. As the spring wore on and his disciplinary time mounted up, he happened to read in the *New York Times* that Prince Rainier and his wife, Princess Grace from Monaco, were planning a visit to the United States in the fall. Jack got the brilliant idea that if they were to come to West Point, the custom would be that they would grant amnesty, and that would forgive all punishments. So, unbeknown to anyone, he wrote them and invited them to come for a football game in the fall. Amazingly, they accepted the invitation, and when they arrived amnesty was granted, and Jack was a free cadet again.

. . Their Serene Highnesses Prince Ranier and Princess Grace attended the football game in Michie Stadium.

Prince Rainier and Princess Grace (Kelly)
going to the football game

In the fall, before each home football game, a pep rally was held Friday night to get the troops riled up. The cadets did not have their own marching band, so the year that I was a senior, I organized a Pep Band. Anyone could play whatever instrument they had, or innovated, and I directed it with a sink plunger. We had no music, and quality was not anything we strived to attain. We just had fun and this added to the football spirit.

Leading the Pep Band with a toilet plunger, in our bath robes

My spiritual devotion never wavered. Although we were required to attend chapel each week, I also joined the chapel choir with a practice each Wednesday evening. I always felt a special peace when in the chapel, but it took another thirty years to realize where such a feeling originated. Singing in a choir of all men was very inspiring by itself!

As predicted by my pre-academy instructors, my academic challenges continued for the entire four years. Fortunately, I was a good enough student in all other subjects to allow for a focus on foreign language and English literature, which were my weakest subjects, although all courses were a struggle. During the last year, just about two weeks before graduation, one of the daily exams in English literature was on the book *1984*. The exam consisted of three parts for a total of 3.0. One part, a third of the grade, was "Give the allegorical significance of (the title of one of the chapters)." I had never heard of the word *allegorical* and, of course, if you didn't know the definition you would never guess what it meant. So much for one unit out of a three-unit grade. For another unit, there were ten names of characters in the book, and we were to describe their part on the narrative. One of them turned out to be mentioned in one sentence in the book—he was a doorman—and most others were also rather obscured characters. I blew this one daily test so badly it threw my average below 2.0, with very little time to make up for it. This provoked another "wash-out" evaluation and, again, I was "restricted to quarters" until the results were known. Of course, my family and many relatives were there waiting for me to be allowed to graduate, and to get married the very next day. As the Lord would have it, I passed this special evaluation, and my new life began. Lord, thank you for having in your plan for me to succeed in this enormous struggle. Thank you, Lord, for the confidence that I have that, with you, I can do all things you led me to. This trust, Lord, will be with me the rest of my life, and I promise to give you all the credit.

During my last year, President Eisenhower was reelected for a second term, and I again participated in the inauguration, this time marching in the parade as a cadet. What a claim-to-fame, being in both of his celebrations during the swearing-in ceremonies. Thank you, Lord, for such memories.

Inaugural Parade...

... finally we had arrived . . . marching down Pennsylvania Avenue . . . passing our Commander in Chief . . .

I always wanted to join the Air Force. The Air Force Academy had only recently opened, and the first graduating class was the year after my graduation from West Point. About 12.5% of our class were allowed to accept a commission in the Air Force, instead of the Army, based upon our class ranking academically. We, of course, did not know our ranking until just before graduation. I was so determined, however, to declare my true desire for the Air Force, whether I could make it or not, that I had my class ring made with an Air Force blue stone and I had it engraved inside with the initials "USAF." My prayers were answered and the Air Force became my new career. Thank you, again, Lord, with my life changing dramatically in such a joyous way.

The wedding was very memorable for all and was attended by all of our aunts and uncles as well as our families. We had reservations for our guests at the Stone Mountain Inn, an inspiring hotel on a nearby mountain overlooking the Hudson River. Our wedding was conducted by the Reverend Fairbanks, a retired Episcopal pastor living in Maine and a very fond friend of the Clark family, who was very honored to conduct a service in this imposing Cadet Chapel. A few years later, when we visited him during his retirement in Maine, he told us that that experience in the West Point Cadet Chapel, he considered it to be the high point in his lifetime ministry.

Lieutenant Dean and Katie Bates under the swards

Cadet Chapel

As I look back on my days at West Point, only the Lord could have orchestrated such a plan. This plan included Herb Woodard for introduction to flying, Cal Canfield my mentor that encouraged my appointment, his wife Barb our matchmaker, with Katie my encourager, my year of preparation courses at Defiance College, my aunt

Leota and Uncle Homer Isley to visit me at my most discouraging time, my academic standing being just good enough to go into the Air Force, and the Lord as my strength and guide. It took me another thirty-two years before I realized that the Lord, *personally*, had faithfully guided these events all along the way. I was able to successfully complete it by devoting myself to do how he has inspired me—to do my best, one day at a time, and leave the results to him. Perseverance and endurance were required on my part. Because I did not realize the Lord knew me personally, he used Katie as the main reason that I did not quit, as she believed in me strongly and was clearly the love of my life. I also would have had to face my family and hometown friends with having given up.

Katie was my daily encourager, and after six years of our continued love and devotion to each other, we were finally married in the beautiful chapel on the hill at West Point, the day after I graduated. What a thrill of accomplishment and what a prize for a wife! I have recently come to realize also was the six years of writing love letters, I could easily express my memories and feelings easily, making this book possible.

We had no money when we were married, but also no debt. We both had a strong spiritual life, with trust that the Lord would be out friend and provider. Although Katie had a special-education teaching degree, her passion was to be a loving wife, a stay-at-home mother, and a grandmother. She willingly lived on our one income and never wished more than what we could afford. Her *only* regret during her last days was that she was not able to see her only great-granddaughter.

> I can only give you love that lasts forever,
> And the promise to be near each time you call.
> And the only heart I own is yours and yours
>   alone,
> That's all, that's all.

I can only give you country walks in springtime,
And a hand to hold when leaves begin to fall,
And a love whose burning light to warm the win-
     ter night,
That's all, that's all.

There are those I am sure who have told you,
They will give you the world for a toy,
All I ask for these arms to enfold you,
And a love time can never destroy.

If you're wondering what I'm asking in return, dear
You'll be glad to know that my demands are
     small.
Say it's me that you'll adore for now and evermore.
That's all, that's all.

          —Bob Haymes and Alan Brant

    (I suggest that you Google "That's All, That's
All" and Select Nat King Cole as the artist.)

Chapter 4

AIR FORCE

After graduating from West Point and a two-month paid honeymoon and vacation, I reported in to the Air Force at Maxwell AFB at Montgomery, Alabama. This assignment was for a two-month course as an introduction to the Air Force while awaiting my assignment to begin basic pilot training in Texas. While there, I learned a very good lesson in our marriage relationship. The apartment complex that we rented had a swimming pool that we could use, but it was at another complex about a mile away. One Sunday afternoon, we put our suits on and drove down for a swim. On the way back, Katie looked over and remarked that we seemed low on gas—don't you think that you should stop at a gas station for gas? My reply was, "If I thought we needed it, I would stop." We didn't go, but another block or so the car stopped. I have eaten these words all these years later.

From Montgomery, we then traveled to the lowest part of Texas, to Moore Air Base near Mission. Thus began my next significant challenge: flight training. To become a pilot, training consisted of two six-month training sessions referred to as basic followed by advance pilot training. My basic training consisted of flights in the T-34, a small Beechcraft for six weeks with remainder of the time spent in the T-28, both of which were propeller-driven aircraft. The T-28 had a large propeller-driven 500 horsepower engine, with the cockpit about ten feet above the ground. It was a lot to handle for a beginning student.

T-28 Trainer during basic flight training

During this time, marriage was wonderful, and Katie taught first grade at a local school. What a challenge she had as many of them were from migrant families that did not arrive from work in the North until well after school began in the fall. They again they left in the spring when work for the parents became available as they migrated North. During our time at Mission, we were delighted to get the news that Katie was pregnant with our dear daughter, Jennifer.

After basic, we were assigned to Greenville AFB in Mississippi for advanced training in the single-engine jet trainer, the T-33. This was the training version of the F-80 Shooting Star, the first jet airplane developed for the Air Force. This airplane was a bit underpowered, had a 350-gallon tip tank on each wing, and had about a one-and-a-half-hour endurance, depending on the maneuvers and altitude flown. During low-altitude flying, this endurance could be cut down to as much as to one hour due to much higher fuel consumption.

This airplane was the one that I spent the most time in during my eight-year career. In the year before I began flying the T-33, the Air Force finally determined why, occasionally, this airplane would blow up on takeoff. Several planes had exploded and pilots had lost their life, but the solution did result in the airplane becoming extremely reliable, and no further such incidents occurred thereafter.

T-33 jet trainer and support airplane

My training was incident-free, but one of my classmates, while flying solo, had to bail out. It was discovered that he had lost control of the aircraft due to severe instability caused by one tip tank being depleted while the other failed to feed. The pilot did not have any indication available to him as to the cause of the instability nor would he have had any way of avoiding the bailout.

As we approached the end of my training, we were asked for our preference for single-engine (instructor or fighter) or for multi-engine (cargo or bomber) aircraft. For the first time, I was faced with the dilemma of a career of killing people and destroying things, or a career in support operations as an instructor or cargo pilot. I enthusiastically requested to become an instructor and, the Lord willing, I was permanently assigned to Webb AFB, Big Spring, Texas, while awaiting an assignment to instructor school.

In the T-33 cockpit upon graduation and getting my wings

Within the first month after arrival in Texas, Katie delivered Jennifer, and a new season in our life began. Unfortunately, we knew no one there to share our joy, but we were thrilled nonetheless. After two months at Big Spring, I was temporarily assigned for the three-month instructor school at Craig AFB, at Selma, Alabama, and then return to Webb AFB for instructing in the T-33. In Selma, there were no apartments to rent for such a short time. I also knew that apartments were scarce in Big Spring. There was no way that I could I be without my newborn sweet little girl and my dear wife. Therefore, I purchased a mobile home that we lived in while in Selma, and then transported it to Big Spring. This arrangement worked out very well, even though it became a bit cramped when Jim came along twenty-one months later, and when Katie's mother came to help with Jim. Such is the life of a military family, and we learn to endure—with God's help.

About six months after becoming an instructor, I was with a student when we got caught air born when an unexpected dust storm hit the base. At that time in the development of weather forecasting, these dust storms were quite unpredictable, and were always (it seemed) coming from a heading ninety degrees to the runway heading, causing a significant crosswind. On this occasion, all airplanes were called back to the base, and I happened to be the last one to return. I was flying from the back seat, which was very challenging due to the front ejection seat in the way, and the plexiglass distorted what view was available from the back seat. When I turned toward the runway for landing the first time, the wind was so strong that we were blown to the side and we had to go around for another approach. This time, I was able to get aligned to the runway with lots of "crab" into the wind. I touched down on one wheel, and as I straightened out the crab, the plane started skipping off toward the side of the runway. I then again put a crab into the wind and skipped down the runway somewhat sideways while I got the flaps up that would secure us to the runway. As a young instructor, there was much anxiety that went with this event. Thank you, Lord, that you saved me, a very young inexperienced instructor.

We purchased a small English car, a four-door Morris Minor (VW size). When the Christmas holidays approached, we planned a trip all the way to our families in Ohio to show off, for the first time, Jennifer our precious new addition to the family. We purchased a canvas baby basket for her that would just fit between the front passenger seat and the back of the back seat. This made it very convenient for Katie to attend to our beautiful baby. (This was before seat belts or children's car seats were invented). When in Ohio and coming from my parents to the farm, a light snow had fallen. When approaching the farm as we turned slightly and went over a bridge, the car started skidding on ice that had built up on the bridge. The car turned one way and then the other way and finally slid backward toward the edge of a steep eight-foot-deep ditch. The car skidded sideways into the grass and the car stopped within inches of rolling over into the ditch. Thank you, Lord, for saving us—especially our little one (two months old) that surely would have been severely injured.

Our 1958 Morris Minor

About a year into my assignment at Webb AFB, I was teaching students how to fly in formation. During the summer heat in Texas, the performance of the T-33 drops somewhat, and the airplane needs to be more tenderly coaxed off the ground during takeoff. One of my students was to fly solo and to lead our formation, while I flew on the wing in the back seat with another of my students in the front. We were on the right side of the lead aircraft, to take off with barely wing-tip clearance, and nose to tail clearance. As we approached takeoff speed, the lead aircraft jerked the nose up too fast, and the airplane stalled as it lifted off the ground. His airplane dropped back to the runway with his right wing low, turning directly in front of our airplane. I grabbed control of our airplane and somehow managed to nurse our plane in the air directly over the lead aircraft. Our airplane went over, just ahead of the other one who was able to get control and continue his takeoff, ending up behind us. Somehow, by the grace of God, our aircraft avoided colliding. Considering that each aircraft had 350 gallons of jet fuel in each of the tip tanks, fuel in the wings and a fuel tank directly behind the rear seats, for a total of 1,880 gallons in the two aircraft, it was an absolute miracle that we did not end up in a big ball of fire at the end of the runway. Thank you, Lord—I guess that it just was not my time for you to take me home.

Part of the training program was for each student to experience a weekend cross-country with four segments. Students, of course, are expected to make mistakes, and they are usually at the most unexpected times. One flight into Davis-Montham AFB at El Paso, TX, the student in the front seat was to make an approach for landing. On the approach, we were too high and I told the student to go around. He thought that he could save the landing, and a debate continued until I told him to see how it would turn out. Unbeknownst to me, during this encounter he had raised the landing gear. The gear handle was located in the front seat and I was not readily aware of it being raised. As a safety check of my own, just before landing, I had developed a habit of rechecking the indicators for the proper position of the flaps, speed brakes, and landing gear. Lo and behold, the indicators for the landing gear showed that they were up, and we were able to initiate a go-around just as we were bringing the nose of the aircraft up for touchdown. Whee! Saved again, thank you, Lord!

For some reason, that escapes me now, I was flying at night alone, returning to the base. We always fly with an oxygen mask, as we needed oxygen when above ten thousand feet. As I was cruising back at an altitude well above thirty thousand feet, my breathing suddenly stopped. I discovered that somehow my oxygen tube had become disconnected and my breathing had sucked up my flight suit in the leg. Had this not have happened, I could have experienced oxygen deprivation with a slow onset of unconsciousness. Whee, saved again!

The T-33 was a very basic airplane with no autopilot, barely adequate heating, no cockpit lighting except for the individual instrument gauges, only two navigation radios that required manual tuning to an AM- and to an FM-type station. During a letdown to an airport, the FM radio had to be changed to the final-approach station. The radio panels were located on the left-side panel with no overhead lighting and needed a flashlight with one hand at night to see while tuning with the other hand. This was going on while the airplane was flying by itself—hands off even though had unstable flight characteristics. Radar (Ground Control Approach [GCA]) was available for most major military bases, but for smaller bases we needed to request an approach radar on our flight plan submitted before takeoff. The Ground Control Approach (GCA) radar provides the ground controller information as to the position of the aircraft relative to the course and glide slope to the runway touchdown. The controller would then talk us down. If the radar was not available, we would have to use the published approach charts from a publication that we would put on our knee clipboard. Reading them at night, again, needed a flashlight, and the information had much detail on a small chart. We would have to manually navigate the aircraft course relative to the published chart information and estimate the glide slope position relative to the runway.

I will never forget my experience with flying into the smog of California before the time that pollution clean-up began. I was flying with a student, and we had stopped for refueling at Williams AFB in Arizona. As we approached California we had beautiful visibility of the ground, Approach Control ask us if we could hold our let-down for a while as there was an emergency in progress. Since we had plenty of fuel we, of course, agreed. They held us at altitude for what seemed longer than we expected, but they finally vectored us down for our approach. I had requested a GCA on the flight plan and again when I contacted Approach Control, and assumed that it would be available. Approach Control vectored us at low altitude for some distance and then advised us that they were terminating their radar control and for us to take over our own navigation to the field. I questioned them regarding a GCA, and they advised that none was available. I had not bothered to tune in the approach radio frequency as I had assumed that the GCA was available. By now we were in very limited visibility due to the smog, the runway was not in sight, too late to dial in the radio frequency, and the low fuel lights came on. Through and above the smog we could see the mountains just to the east of George AFB on the heading we were taking, and I told the student to look around to try to spot the field. Suddenly he said that he could see the runway a short way off to the left, and we a 180-degree turn and landed uneventfully, with all three low-fuel lights shining. Whee! You saved me again, my Lord!

In February of 1981, I volunteered to take a flight to Vermont with the Base Maintenance director, a full-colonel. He was not a pilot and needed this flight to coordinate maintenance requirements for the aircraft that were being transferred to Webb AFB. En route to Vermont, we refueled at Little Rock, Arkansas, for the long flight to Vermont. By the time we reached Vermont, it had become dark. I was the only pilot and, of course, had requested a GCA upon arrival. When I contacted Approach Control, I again requested a GCA and was then advised that none was available, and I was to use my published approach to the field. I was also advised that visibility was reduced due to light snowstorm. I had the approach chart on my knee board but, of course, I had to fly the airplane while studying the chart with my flashlight and tuning in the radio stations of which there were two that were required for the approach. In making my published letdown, as I turned to the approach heading and dialed in the final radio station, the course indicator showed full-scale deflection. I, therefore, had no way of knowing how far off course and, correspondingly, where the field was. I immediately declared an emergency and within moments a voice came on indicating that they now had me on radar and started giving me course corrections. We, of course, had been flying at low altitude and burning up fuel like crazy. By the time we landed, all three low-fuel warning lights were on. In considering how fortunate we were to be on the ground safely, we also came to realize that we were wearing summer flight clothing, and the difficulty of ever finding us in the mountains of Vermont in the night and in the snow was daunting. In retrospect, I discovered that the published approach was slightly non-standard in a way that I had overlooked. Whee! Lord, you saved me again. How did the radar controller suddenly become available at the exact time that I needed him, with the equipment turned on, warmed up, and calibrated? Obviously your miraculous intervention to save me!

For one of the class graduation ceremonies, my squadron commander, a lieutenant colonel, was assigned to conduct the flyby. He organized a sixty-four-airplane formation that was unique. This formation was of a diamond shape, consisting of a total of sixty-four aircrafts. All went well for the flyby, and then he took us up to altitude and put us all into a trail position, one behind another for a long string of sixty-four airplanes. He then did the unthinkable by doing a loop. The T-33 by itself was able to perform a loop if you kept it tight. However, in trail position, each subsequent airplane had to fly a slightly larger loop until part way through the maneuver aircraft were stalling out and falling out of position causing severe chaos. Fortunately and amazingly, none of the aircraft collided, but there were four airplanes that were found to have been overstressed beyond the design limit for G-forces. Another spectacular save, Lord—thank you!

After two years instructing, I was offered the opportunity of attending the Squadron Officer's School (SOS) at the Air University, and we relocated back to Maxwell AFB in Alabama. This was a three-month course for career officers, but a very intense and demanding course of study for me. By this time, we had our family blessed with Jim with two children under three years old. The only living quarters available for short-term rental was a double-wide mobile home. This was a very stressful time for us due to the demands of my course, my need for quiet study time in the evenings, two children and their commotion in a mobile home, and to top it off…Katie found out that she was again pregnant. In addition, I received an assignment to Ramstein AFB in Germany for three years. Therefore, at the conclusion of SOS, I took Katie and the kids to Ohio to stay at the farm, while I returned to Webb for a few days to pack up what we could ship to Germany and to dispense of the rest. I went to Ohio for a few days, and then proceeded on to Ramstein alone, as I had to locate living accommodations before Katie and the family could come. It took two months to locate and rent a home, in small country town called Mehlboch. When Katie and the family came, she had the task of flying from Detroit to Philadelphia, to change planes and then on to Newark, New Jersey. From there, she had to take a bus to McGuire AFB. At McGuire, she and the kids boarded an Air Force transport for a flight to London, and then on to Frankfort, Germany, where I met them. This was a daunting experience for Katie with two very small children, traveling approximately thirty-six hours with virtually no sleep, six months pregnant, and incredibly no one ever offered to help her. Such hardships military families are expected to endure and get very little credit for. The wives of military personnel are to be honored for the many great sacrifices they must make in support of their husband's career, and for family unity. I thank the Lord for my dear wife, Katie—she endured honorably!

The month that I arrived in Germany was the month that the Russians began building the famous Berlin Wall, the Iron Curtain, and escalating the Cold War. I was again assigned to fly the T-33 in support of airbase requirements, to provide check rides of personnel assigned to the 17th Air Force Headquarters, to act as decoys for fighter training, and to conduct a monthly flying school refresher course for all flying personnel, of which there were three fighter squadrons on base. Flights were often flown throughout Western Europe, England, and as far south as Northern Africa. Each country had subscribed to a standard set of flight rules except for France, who insisted on having their own. They required that, before entering their air space, we were to contact them for permission to enter and for receiving our altitude assignment. France was never very cooperative and always required us to alter our altitude upon entering their airspace. The closest East German boarder was about eighty miles due east of Ramstein, which made the airspace very congested with both military and commercial aircraft. The flying situation was compounded by much rain, overcast conditions, some snow, and operations were conducted at night as well as day. The navigational aids were antiquated, compared with current facilities, and often rather unreliable. What the Russians did to aggravate relations was to place an identical navigational radio facility just across the border, set the same frequencies as ours, and crank up the power. In this way, they might cause our aircraft to stray across the border, and they would then shoot them down. This situation persisted throughout the time that I was at Ramstein. Finally, there were enough aircraft lost to justify the Pentagon directing that all flights in Europe cease operations until an inspection team was sent over to review all operations before they were cleared to fly again. This happened only four months before we returned to the U.S. During one of my flights I experienced such a diversion that confused me and I had the feeling that I should turn west. This I did until I reoriented myself, and it turned out that I was ready to enter the boarder of the Air Defense Identification Zone (ADIZ) that was ten miles from the east Border. At jet speeds, I was very close to being a statistic. Thank you, Lord, for saving me from this potential of being shot down.

In November 1963, one of our pilots in the support squadron and another pilot was reported missing. It was subsequently discovered that they had crashed their T-33, and there were no survivors. That evening we invited our friends, Al and Sandy St. Marie, to come over to our home to reflect on the demise of our mutual friends. When they arrived at our apartment, they burst in the door and said that they just heard on the radio that President Kennedy had been shot and killed. Double sorrow in one day.

Stanley, our third child, was born in the nearby Army hospital at Landstule, Germany. What a gift from God he has been for us, and he and Suzie, his wife, have been fully committed Christians.

About halfway through my assignment to Ramstein, I was selected to become an instructor in the newest support airplane, the twin engine T-39. This was an executive-type airplane that seated two pilots plus five passengers. This program was developed to train selected pilots from other air bases throughout Europe, to be checked out to fly their new aircraft when they were delivered. This was a very nice performing airplane, pressurized so that supplemental oxygen was not required, and we did not have to wear parachutes or oxygen masks. What a pleasure! One evening after dark, I was instructing a pilot in touch-and-go landings. After one landing and just as we added power for another takeoff, a deer came into our headlights directly in front of us. I grabbed the controls, jammed full power, and was just barely able to lift up over the deer. If we would have hit the deer, this would have been very serious as the nose wheel would have collapsed at a speed of over 120 knots. Another thank-you, Lord, for my being able to avoid such a collision.

T-39 Saberliner executive jet

Throughout my flying career and after all of the near-misses that I have experienced, I never developed a fear for the next flight. Interestingly enough, although I had a fear of being on a ladder on the ground, I only once had a fear of heights in the cockpit. I was on a flight in a T-33, over the English Channel and above thirty thousand feet on a beautiful clear day. The other pilot had the controls, and I gazed over the side toward the water. I spotted a freighter ship below and watched it for a while. How very small it looked and I thought how high we were to make it so small. I then realized that about a foot below my feet was the bottom of the airplane, and there was nothing below that but air. Wow! Time to concentrate on the land ahead of us and ignore the ship.

At the end of our assignment, I received orders back to Maxwell AFB, Alabama, to Base Operations. During the entire three-year assignment, Katie and the kids were not able to return to the U.S. Five days before departure, Jim came down with a case of measles. We already had our flight reservations, but if he was not healed enough, we would have to delay our departure. What a great disappointment this would have been, but the last day before departure, his spots had faded enough that the doctor gave us a release. More thanks to you, Lord!

During our assignment to Maxwell AFB, I was able to be checked out not only in the T-33 but also in a WWII C-47 cargo airplane. In addition I got checked out in the small twin-engine Aero Commander. This was a light cargo plane designated the U-4 capable of carrying four passengers. One day, I was assigned to take a flight by myself to the Meridian Naval Air Station, Mississippi, in the U-4. This was a once-a-month trip for the purpose of purchasing several cases of liquor from their Officers Club. Alabama was a "dry state," meaning that no alcohol could be purchased. Maxwell was where the Air University was located, with a number of high-ranking officers who liked to party. As a result, a program was developed whereby they could call their liquor orders in to Base Operations, and we would fly over to provide pickup and delivery services. I flew over by myself, about a one-hour trip, purchased and loaded several cases of liquor. On takeoff, as I rotated the nose of the aircraft, for some reason the seat released suddenly moving me back so far that I could not reach the control wheel. As the airplane proceeded to takeoff by itself, I rapidly released my seatbelt and shoulder harness, leaned forward on my knees, and grabbed the wheel to regain control and fly to a safe altitude where I could reposition my seat. Being able to recover from such a serious potential disaster was clearly a blessing from you, Lord!

During the winter months, I volunteered to help deliver a refurbished C-47 from Miami to Tripoli, Libya. The airplane had been totally overhauled and was being given to the Libyan government as part of the Military Assistance Program. The C-47 was a twin-engine cargo plane, designed before WWII, and had been a workhorse for many years. The commercial version was the first passenger airplane, designated the DC-3. This airplane did not have deicing capability for flying the northern route to Europe, so extra fuel tanks were to be installed in order to have range enough to fly the southern route. There was no pressurization and no oxygen, and the airplane was designed to be low (below ten thousand feet) and slow (less than 200 mph). I was designated the copilot and met the pilot at the airplane in Miami. We flew to Charleston, SC, for the fuel tanks to be installed and to meet up with the navigator. All went well for two days before we departed on the first over-water leg to Bermuda. I had never flown with a navigator before, and his primary source for navigation was a sextant mounted in a Plexiglas bubble projecting above the top of the airplane. After an hour or so, I called him and ask how he was doing. He said that he would call back in a few minutes. When he did so, he advised that he had discovered a problem, that the compass ring mounted around the sextant had not been calibrated. He said that was okay, however, as he aligned it with the tail of the airplane. This didn't do much for my confidence in having to rely on him to find our way over water, and I continued with my basic "time and distance" calculations as we proceeded to Bermuda. We did find the island without incident, primarily as it was not a long flight. In Bermuda, we stayed two days for R & R. We rented motor scooters to tour the island and somehow survived driving on the left side of the road with only one incident. While exiting a roundabout, a bus was approaching and we got confused to the point of stopping directly in front of the bus driver, who also stopped, and he smiled as we finally determined which side of the bus to go around. Our next flight was to the Azores, a small group of islands off the west coast of Africa. This was to be a very long eleven-hour flight, ending in the dark around eleven o'clock. As we proceeded, I was still anxious with having to depend solely on the navigator. The pilot, however, said that I should give up on it as, if we were one-fourth degree off course, we would never see the island. The navigator did his job, and we found the island without delay. There was little to see on the island, so after a day's rest we proceeded on to Madrid, Spain. By this time we needed another two days of rest (to visit the city), and then pressed on to Libya, one-day's flight. After an overnight's rest in Libya and completing the paperwork, we boarded a commercial flight to London and on to New York. We were back to the US in one day, after taking eleven days going over. Thank you, Lord, for keeping us safe from such an intimidating journey.

WWII C-47 like one we flew to Libya North Africa

When President Kennedy had been killed and replaced by Lyndon Johnson, who was very unpopular, and his secretary of defense was Robert MacNamara who had no military experience, they were obviously heading us for a war in Vietnam. At that time we had three children and I was three years over my military obligation, so I decided to resign from the Air Force. I submitted my resignation in February 1965 and it was soon accepted for separation in May. Within a month of resignation, all other requests were denied as we were about to officially enter the military conflict in Vietnam. Thank you, Lord—I just made it out in time!

My next dilemma was what career to take in civilian life. I believe that this is a great challenge to all military personnel when they depart, especially officers. They may have had a successful and extensive career of managing military personnel and responsibilities, but nothing that directly translates into a civilian career. In my case, I could have flown for any of the airlines who were hiring all available pilots, but I was ready to get out of the cockpit. I had a desire for management, and to be able to stay closer to home with the family.

In looking back at my Air Force experiences, it is very clear that the Lord had been with me all the way, saving me from all those potential disasters. Did I realize at the time that he was there faithfully saving me? No. Did I ever thank him for his grace in putting Katie in my life to create such a loving family? No. In my defense, we faithfully attended church and participated in most related activities. However, in all of our church attendance, I never came to realize that the Lord was in on all our thoughts, words, and actions—every day in every way since I asked him into my life. It took me another twenty-five years before I was brought to a realization that he has been faithful to me, even though I have not been faithful in return.

> Great is Thy faithfulness, O God my Father.
> There is no shadow of turning with Thee
> Thou changest not, Thy compassions they fail not,
> Great is Thy faithfulness. Lord unto me.
>
> Great is Thy faithfulness, great is Thy faithfulness,
> Morning by morning new mercies I see.
> All I have needed Thy hand hath provided,
> As Thou hast been, Thou forever will be
>
> —Thomas Chisholm
>
> (I suggest that you Google "Great Is Thy Faithfulness" and listen to Chris Rice.)

Lord, the amazing thing that I often reflect on is that, despite these potential disasters that you saved me from, you have helped me avoid any fear of the future. You gave me an adventurer's spirit that I still have to this day, to do what others may fear to try. And yet, that is where I can see you along side of me, protecting, guiding, encouraging me and giving me a special sense of joy, peace, and courage to carry on with enthusiasm.

Webster's definition of enthusiasm, before changed to be politically correct, included…endowed with the Holy Spirit…

Chapter 5

LIVING IN PENNSYLVANIA AND NEW YORK

Leaving the Air Force after eight years in addition to the four years of military life at the academy created a huge dilemma—where do I fit into a civilian career? I have now come to realize that this is a common obstacle for nearly all military personnel, especially officers. In my case, I could have been employed by any of the airlines, as they were begging for pilots during that period of time due to the rapid introduction of jets into their fleet. However, I was ready to get out of the cockpit and into a job whereby I could use my desire for management responsibilities, and to be home more for the family. I, therefore, accepted a job as a copilot for a small manufacturing company near Williamsport, PA. This company was just taking delivery of a new Beechcraft Queen Air and wanted a copilot to assist the pilot that they had for years. This airplane was a very nice executive airplane, twin engine propeller driven, and pressurized so that it could fly at median altitudes, between ten thousand feet and twenty thousand feet. The aircraft accommodated a total of six people, including flight crew. My employment agreement was with the understanding that I would fly as copilot while transitioning into a position in the company management. Unfortunately, I found the flying to be quite demanding, and the company never was interested in my management desires. The copilot job required early morning departures taking company management out for business meetings.

Typically, our job as pilots was to be at the airport early enough to bring the coffee and donuts, check on weather, file a flight plan, bring the airplane out of the hanger, refuel it, and pre-flighted before the passengers arrived. After flying to a destination, we then stayed around the airport for the day and flew back after the day's meetings were concluded. I was never invited to attend the meetings in order to learn the business. After arrival at Williamsport, we had to put the airplane away for the night, and we then would arrive home in late evening. The next day would be more of the same.

In the middle of the winter, we had three clients from South Africa that visited our plant in Pennsylvania, and we were then to take them to a small airport in Canada. In my employment agreement, I had agreed to fly as a copilot as long as I could overrule the pilot's decision in the event that I considered the operation too dangerous. When we approached this small airport, the visibility was low due to a light snowstorm. The airport did not have a control tower or any approach navigational aids of any kind. The pilot, Bob, was a seat-of-your-pants type of pilot and wanted to let down and give it a try to see if we could find the field. I strongly objected and stated that if he wanted to try, he could take me to Toronto, which was nearby, and let me out before proceeding. Fortunately, he accepted my position. When I announced this situation to the passengers, they were in total agreement with us going to Toronto. When on the ground, they informed us that in South Africa, their president and two other senior officers recently lost their lives in a plane crash at home, so were pleased with our decision to divert.

Beechcraft guaranteed that the Queen Air carburetors would not ice up during winter operations, which would cut off fuel to the engines during certain temperature and moisture conditions. We were returning from another flight to Canada during the winter and were in the middle of New York State, in clouds and in the dark. Suddenly, both engines sputtered and quit. We established a glide, and believed that we had experienced carburetor icing. The plane was equipped with intake doors that we could close manually with pull-out knobs, in order to allow heat from the engine to melt the ice. We frantically closed these doors and, fortunately, soon we were able to restart the engines. Thank you, Lord, for being with us in these conditions and saving us from a potential disaster.

After one year, I discovered a large flight simulator company, Singer-Link, that had built the Link Trainers for training WWII pilots. This device was prominent during this war as all military pilots needed to learn to fly in clouds and at night. I was fortunate to have met Ed Link personally just before he died. Mr. Link developed this trainer using technology that his father had adopted to build large theater organs

Singer-Link was growing rapidly to meet the training needs of the rapidly expanding airline crews. This company was located about one hundred miles away, and I was soon offered a job in the sales department.

WWII Link trainer used to teach all pilots
to fly without visual references

The Singer sewing machine company purchased the Link Company just before I joined them in 1966. It was growing rapidly to meet the training needs of the airlines, as they were just entering the jet age of airline travel. The position I accepted was as a sales engineer with commercial airlines as my clients. I was assigned to represent the company with all airlines in the western part of the country. My first trip was to United Airlines in Denver, CO, traveling with my boss, the director of airline sales. This visit turned out to be a challenging one in that United had taken delivery of a few of our simulators and still had a number of problems with them. More serious, however, was that they had issued a detailed request for proposal for another simulator, and Singer-Link had responded with a standard proposal that ignored United's specific requirements. After the meeting, I was sent home with four days to clarify our intentions in providing for these specific requirements. We, of course, lost the contract to a competitor, and I learned a big lesson regarding the need to customize our proposals to meet the stated requirements of the customer. Based on this experience, I designed a way to resolve this issue for future proposals. For the next two years, however, a number of sales were lost because of operational and maintenance complaints with our delivered simulators. Such complaints started with the in-plant acceptance testing that was extended because the simulators were not ready when the customer was called in for their evaluations. As a result, I eventually moved to head up the Final Assembly Quality Control Department. I began to evaluate the simulators in detail as they were being prepared for in-plant customer acceptance. This is where I could use my flying experience to identify problems, in addition to the detailed acceptance criteria. This effort cut our customer acceptance testing by a few weeks which, in turn, reduced customer frustration and associated costs for our company.

Problems with the simulators that were already delivered continued to be evident. After some time, I then moved to become manager of the customer support department, supporting our simulators worldwide. I inherited a group of about a dozen highly skilled technicians and, as time went by, this grew to about twenty. I can now look back and realize that the Lord orchestrated this position for me, as it uniquely used all of my skills of the past along with my desired for management responsibilities. I had the flying and flight training experience, the people skills to interface with the customers, the engineering knowledge to understand the highly technical nature of the simulators, and I enjoyed the management challenges. As a part of motivating my employees and encouraging a willingness to jump on to the next airplane to meet customer requirements, I helped invent flexible working hours. When they returned from a very demanding trip to get the customer back into operation, I would reward them with a few days off. I developed a program for performing modifications and updates, and to relocate simulators as they were resold to other airlines. The relationship with my employees was very good. None of them wanted my job, and I couldn't do theirs, but I was familiar enough technically that I could manage these programs.

The needs for our services took us throughout the world: England, France, Germany, the Netherlands, Sweden, Finland, South Africa, Ethiopia, Kenya, Jordan, India, Pakistan, Japan, and Australia as well as all over the United States. In order to answer our incoming customer calls for help during off-hours, we subscribed to an answering service whereby an operator would answer the call, place the customer on hold, and start down the list of employees in our department. I was first on the list for thirteen years, and calls could be expected during weekends, holidays, and even in the middle of the night. We would discuss the customer needs, and then do our best to get them back in operation as soon as possible. As the years went by, I came to realize that somehow a solution to their needs would always be found; often within a few hours or day, but well within one week—sometimes in the most unusual ways. It was important to not panic, and keep exploring options that would lead to a solution to their problem. I would often state this awareness to others, that there was *always* a solution. This realization came about years before I was aware that the Lord was working 24-7 in my behalf, to help find a way out of every situation.

During the thirteen years that I managed the customer support department, customer satisfaction did improve considerably and we were able to gain back our good reputation. All of the foreign airlines would provide free first-class tickets for all of our business travels. In order to help justify and fund our technical staff, I developed a modification program to update software, modify hardware, install visual systems, and relocate simulators as the need arose. This program worked well, as it gave some in-plant work for my employees awaiting the next time they were needed in the field, as well as to provide much needed assistance to our customers.

This modification program would occasionally include work on competitor's simulators after they had gone out of business. In this regard, we took on a contract with Pan American Airways (PAA) at JFK Airport in New York, to replace the motion system on an older competitor's simulator. This simulator was built using a set of long hydraulic cylinders that suspended the cockpit from a very large overhead steel overhead structure. The system had never worked well and required much maintenance. This was a 747 simulator that was critically needed for training. We eventually entered into a contract for replacing this deficient device with our standard motion system, where the cockpit was supported from below. This was a very challenging job, not only from a physical aspect but all the cables leading into the cockpit needed to be replaced. The program went very well and cooperation with PAA was excellent. We had an installation team of four very experienced mechanics to disassemble the old and install the new system. Our mechanics were non-union employees while the PAA maintenance personnel were strongly union, especially at JFK airport. As a favor to us, PAA provided hardhats and coveralls for our people, so that they could blend in easily with the airline personnel. Cooperation between the two groups was excellent, as they needed us and we were well-paid by them. To begin the disassembly, the cables were disconnected and the cockpit set aside. The overhead structure then was to be taken down. When the top frame was lifted off, which probably weighed nearly a ton, for some reason the cable that was lifting the frame using an overhead crane came unwrapped and the frame came crashing to the floor. As it came down, a corner of the frame grazed the side of the hardhat of one of our employees and pushed him aside just enough to keep the frame from hitting his body. Otherwise, no one or anything was damaged. Needless to say, this drew a crowd, especially of union supervisors and managers from the Port Authority of New York, as well as PAA. The investigation that followed was quietly conducted and we were able to continue with our work without any delay. Amazing that there were no repercussions and that no one was injured. A thousand thanks to you, Lord, for your perfect plan for this event.

As the airlines purchased new aircrafts, they often sold the older airplanes to another airline, along with their simulator. Our little department took on several relocations as well as modifications that might be necessary. One such relocation was a Boeing 720 simulator from PAA in San Francisco to Ethiopian Airlines in Addis Ababa. When I was invited to form a proposal for this project, I was aware that Ethiopia was in some type of political turmoil, but news was nearly impossible to obtain. I contacted the U.S. Embassy in Addis Ababa and was informed that it was safe for Americans. I took a volunteer contract administrator from Singer-Link, and we headed for Ethiopia for discussions with the airline and to assess the situation. Upon arrival, we were met by the chief pilot, Captain Moon, who had been with the airline for many years. He was a TWA pilot and was there under a long-term contract along with six other pilots. He assured us that everything was safe, especially for Americans who were loved by the people. There was, however, political strife as the Communists had taken over the country and eliminated the beloved king, Haille Salassy, about a year prior. Upon arrival on Sunday morning, we were taken to the Hilton Hotel, the largest building in the city at ten stories. As we checked in, there was no one in sight except the clerk, who handed us each a newspaper, the *Ethiopian Herald*, that was folded over. When we opened it up, we were faced with the headline in large block letters: U.S. MILITARY GIVEN FIVE DAYS TO DEPART ETHIOPIA

Needless to say, the next morning early, we visited the U.S. Embassy. They advised us that the directive was only for the military, and it was safe for civilians to remain. The embassy, as well as the airline, encouraged us to proceed with the relocation as it was really needed by the airline, and it would leave a positive reminder of American support for the country. The airline was not influenced by the government, as it played a vital role in contacts with the outside world. I clarified with the airline that I needed to return for a review with my management before a final decision could be made. I was strongly in support of the project and convinced our company to proceed with the contract.

The simulator was disassembled in San Francisco, transported by ship to Djibouti in the Gulf of Aden, and then trucked five hundred miles to Addis Ababa. That meant that the simulator had to be transported up over five thousand feet through mountainous terrain. A few months later, we were informed that the equipment had arrived. I decided to travel alone to evaluate the building that had been built, and become updated as to the political climate. I had still not been able to find any current information on the government situation, but thought that I would try the bookstore at the London airport. When there, I still could not find anything on Ethiopia. I needed some reading material, so I purchased the book *One Flew over the Cuckoo's Nest*. When flying down, there was only one person, a woman, in the first class section of the airplane with me. During a stop in Athens, we conversed and I explained my frustration at not being able to find out about the situation in Ethiopia. It turns out that she was the wife of a diplomat assigned to our embassy in Addis, and she had a copy of a highly sensitive book called *Ethiopia: The Country that Cut Off Its Head*. She let me read it but I was not to show it to anyone on the airplane as it was banned, and I was to give it back before landing in Addis. It was exactly what I needed as it was written by a correspondent for the London Times, who had lived in Ethiopia for many years until he was recently forced out of the country. I read it well into the night and after some time, a flight attendant stopped by for a friendly chat. I was next to the window and she sat on the arm of the aisle seat and said that it must be a very interesting book that I was reading and asked what it was about. I said that it was information about the history of Ethiopia, and that I was interested in the country. Nothing else was said about the book, and later in the flight I finished it and slipped it back to the lady. Upon landing, I was met by Capt. Moon, and while waiting for the baggage, we leaned against a bar on which I laid the "Cuckoo" book upside down. As we were talking, a man walked up to us, reached across us, and picked up the book. He never said a word, looked the book over from front to back, laid it down, and departed. The flight attendant had, obviously, informed communist authorities. The last laugh, however, was mine thinking what the representative must have reported about my "Cuckoo" book. Thank you, Lord, that I was not detained by the communist authorities!

I returned to Binghamton and subsequently informed the airline that we would proceed with the installation. At the Friday dinner table with my parents visiting from Ohio, suddenly the left side of my face became paralyzed. I could not blink my eye, when I drank any liquid it would seep out, my smile was crooked, and it was obvious that something was seriously wrong. The next morning, I went to our family doctor and he diagnosed the condition as Bell's palsy. He said that nothing could be done about it, but said that I needed to manually blink the eyelid to provide lubricant to the eye, and to manually massage my cheek to help keep the muscles working. I informed him that I was slated to go to Ethiopia on Monday, and he said that it was okay but he wanted to see me upon return. I took four technicians with me, and upon arrival, we were again met by Capt. Moon who invited us to his home for a reception with his friends later in the afternoon.

When we arrived, the first person that he introduced me to said, "You have a case of Bell's palsy. How long have you had it?"

I told him since last Friday, and he then asked, "What are you doing about it?"

I told him my doctor said that nothing could be done.

He then said, "That is not true. I want you to come to my office tomorrow morning, and I will read to you out of the medical encyclopedia, a description of what causes it and what can be done."

It turns out, amazingly, that he was from Yugoslavia, had worked his way out from behind the Iron Curtain to Switzerland, worked his way through medical school, and instead of an internship, he accepted a program to go to a third-world country and practice medicine for two years. From the encyclopedia, which was written in German, he translated the material regarding Bell's palsy. It turned out that he was fluent in four languages. He was enjoying his practice, since about every kind of old-time disease that he had studied about in medical school was there in the persons that he treated. He had what was needed to treat Bell's palsy, cortisone and a series of vitamin B supplements, and started them immediately. In two weeks, when I returned to the U.S., approximately 80 percent of the symptoms had gone away, and progress eventually continued until all symptoms disappeared. What a miracle to have healing available to me in Ethiopia through such unusual circumstances. I stagger to think that if I was not treated, the effects would have been devastating to my smile and personality, of which defines me. Thank you, Lord, for miraculously arranging for a doctor to heal my illness in Ethiopia, of all places, when a U.S. doctor could not.

I have always enjoyed the confidence of doing things that others may consider unthinkable. Our family lived on a very tight budget as Katie was a happy, stay-at-home mother. One of our bizarre adventures was a ski and camping trip to Vermont in the winter. We all had about two years of skiing near Binghamton, and I thought that it would be fun to go to Vermont for a weekend of skiing. I had purchased an older, and very small, hardtop camping trailer that I refurbished. It had a small double bed for Katie and me, a bunk bed above for Jennifer, and the boys could sleep on the fold-down table. It had a two-burner cooking stove, a very small closet, and that was about all. We had heating blankets to keep warm, for the trailer was not insulated for winter. I had found a campsite that allowed winter camping near where we wanted to ski, and I made reservations for a late-night Friday check-in. As usual, we left after work and drove up, arriving about ten o'clock that evening. I had been instructed to just find a location and check in in the morning. We arrived and located a site in the park that was part of a farm. Not surprising, we were the only ones in the park. It was very cold when we set up, but soon jumped into our heated beds. The next morning, we woke up to all the walls in the camper covered with frost. I jumped out of bed long enough to get the two gas burners started, and then back in bed until the camper warmed up…somewhat. What we discovered was that it had been a minus eighteen degrees the previous night, and the high for the day would be ten degrees above, with a strong wind. When we got to the ski slope, we found that there were two chair lifts to get us to the top—after riding the lower one, we were to get off and then take the upper one to the top. The problem was that, due to the wind factor, the upper chair lift was closed to prevent possible frostbite. That was okay with us. The entire weekend was a fun adventure, full of memories, and without any problems or issues. Thank you, Lord, for helping us experience such a memorable adventure!

Our winter skiing camping trailer

Another crazy adventure was when the older kids were early to mid-teens, and Bob was approaching one year old. I recognized and discussed at the dinner table one evening that it had been unfortunate that we had not been able to visit any of the states in the west. I proposed that I would take a three-week vacation, get all necessary camping gear, and head west for such an adventure. Everybody agreed (as if they had a choice—I don't remember Katie's reaction). I took our small boat trailer and modified it to have a bottom and sides, open on top to accommodate all our camping gear and luggage. I purchased the largest tent that I could find. Someone donated a handy compact wooden kitchen set of drawers and dish storage. We added a camping stove, ice chests, sleeping bags, lawn chairs, cots and whatever, and covered it over with a tarp. For Bob, I took a portable wooden playpen and cut it down to fit into the back of our big Mercury station wagon, where he could play and sleep. This, obviously, was in the days before seatbelts, child restraints, and such regulations. The other three kids' ages were twelve, fourteen, and Jennifer was sixteen and a half.

In preparation for this trip, I organized a family reunion of Katie's family, to meet in Yellowstone National Park and camp for five days. Most of her family were living on the West Coast, except for her sister Barb and husband Cal, in Ohio. They borrowed a motor home from a relative and drove out for the first Clark family reunion.

Jennifer had obtained her driver's license, and I allowed her to drive as much as she wanted to on the trip. I'm a very trusting soul and confident that I taught her well. As a result, she ended up driving nearly two-third of the seven thousand miles that we traveled. I would usually set in the back seat as it showed my confidence in Jennifer, and I would read a book or take a nap. When we headed out of Binghamton, we headed south to the Interstate that would then take us west. I was reading the newspaper when I suddenly realized that Jennifer had missed the turnoff to go west, and instead was headed east to New York City. No big deal, but this incident has been the source of much laughter through the years. Although the car had over ninety thousand miles on it when we left, we had no problems at all throughout the trip. We drove to Ohio to Barb and Cal's farm, and then to Denver to visited friends from our Air Force days. From there, we headed to the Grand Canyon, to Las Vegas, and on to Yellowstone. After the reunion, we went to Mount Rushmore, and back to New York via the northern route, stopping at Niagara Falls. Although Katie had some genuine second thoughts during the first part of the trip—especially as Bob did not want to sleep or give us a break during the day—she did endure and ultimately enjoyed the adventure. Seeing her families from the West Coast as well as all the sights and experiences, was worth the struggles for her. The car performed very well, especially for the high mileage (for those days), going up Pikes Peak in a snowstorm one day, and through Death Valley desert a few days later. We made it through the desert, in July, during the day in the car that had no air conditioner—surviving on two bags of chipped ice and cold wash cloths.

Two days later, we were in Yellowstone, and found the temperatures below freezing at night. Surprise! We were ill-prepared, but survived. The first morning when Bob woke up, I got up with him and went to warm his bottle in a pan that I had prepared with water the night before, and discovered that the water was frozen solid. What to do? I took Bob in the car and headed out for a drive, allowing the rest of the families to sleep in. I warmed the bottle using the bottle warmer that we that plugged into the cigarette lighter in the car. Bob and I drove around, with him in my arms, seeing the sights around Yellowstone, for about an hour and a half. This, then, became our routine. After four days, we all decided that we would cut the reunion short due to the cold. When we drove out of the park, Jennifer was driving again, with me not paying attention in the back seat. After about an hour we saw a sign reading "Welcome to Montana." Instantly, we knew that a turnoff was missed but not far back. More laughs for the future. Thank you, Lord, for keeping us safe on this adventure and without troublesome issues, while providing memories that none of us will ever forget (except Bob).

Our old Morris Minor car that we purchased in Texas was shipped to Germany for the three years that we were there. Katie really liked the car, so we brought it back to the states. That was the third trip across the Atlantic as it was originally manufactured in England. It was primarily Katie's car. When we had teenage drivers in high school, they would like to occasionally drive to school. So, I found another used Morris that was a wooden body station wagon that I refurbished and painted it red. Needless to say, Jennifer and Jim enjoyed driving it!

The Morris Minor Woody

All our three older kids consider Binghamton their growing-up home. Upon graduation from high school, Jenny went off to Connecticut for college and graduated with a BA in business, married, and has made a home, family, and career in the Hartford area. She now has three beautiful daughters that are living in the New England states. Thank you, Lord, you endowed Jenny with a devoted, loving, and caring heart.

As he grew up, Jim showed an inclination toward mechanical things, and liked to be with me while I was fixing things at home. When I was innovating on a project, he enjoyed reviewing what I planned to do. He would often make suggestions that was helpful and would occasionally catch me at a mistake. He also liked to design things. When he was about eight, he wanted to design and build a boat. So, I gave him the go-ahead, and he designed a flat-bottomed boat with a sloping bow, four feet wide and eight feet long. We proceeded to build it, and it was named *Ark II*. We took it on the Finger Lakes in New York, and we even took it in and around a marina on

Lake Ontario, using a small motor that we borrowed. It was a fun project, doing it together. When he was eleven years old, in recognition of his design interests, for Christmas we gave him a small drawing board. For the next few years, we both ended up using it. When he graduated from high school, he went off to college majoring in architecture, and graduated from Kent State University in Ohio. This has now been his career and is recognized as being a prominent architect in Michigan.

Jim also loved sailing. When he turned fourteen one summer, he went off for a two-week sailing adventure on a seventy-five-foot square-rigged sailboat with a sailing school out of Toronto, Canada. He was courageous enough to travel from Binghamton to Buffalo, get across to Canada, and on to the marina in Toronto. During his birthday celebration on-board, the twenty-three-year-old Skipper gave him the day off from crew duty during their voyage, but he was required to go to the top of both masts and out on each yardarms, to oil each pulley. He has enjoyed sailing on a racing boat for years, and now has a beautiful thirty-six-foot sailboat, cruising in and around upper Lake Huron. What a loving, courageous, and talented son he has been. Thank you, Lord, for his talent and blessing in our lives.

Stan was always a joy as a son, loving, friendly to everybody, and very social. When he was fourteen, he sought out and received a one-year appointment to be a Rotary Club exchange student to Germany, where he was born. He became fluent in the language, made many friends while there, and I am sure he represented America honorably. He joined the high school swim team as a diver and did so well that he was accepted to the Air Force Academy as a diver as well as a well-rounded young man with diverse experiences. Upon graduation from the academy, he has gone on to become an Air Force fighter pilot in the F-16, retired as a lieutenant colonel with twenty-eight years active duty, and now has twenty years as a pilot for Southwest Airlines. Thank you, Lord, for such a spectacular son, who is a devoted believer in you.

After thirteen years of managing the highly stressful customer support department, with its dynamics requiring much unpaid overtime and extensive travel, I found that I had no other choice but to leave the company in order to get away from the job. Each year, all employees received a formal annual performance evaluation, and I was always judged very favorably. For all of this time, I worked for and, therefore, evaluated by a vice president. For the last four or five years of my evaluations, I had requested that I be considered for a position somewhere else in the company, but nothing was ever offered. I was told that I had to have trained someone to replace me before I could expect another position. Due to the demands of the position, no one was willing to consider my job. I would then plea my case to the president who took the same position. As "luck" would have it, (really?) at that time, a simulator company from Tampa, Florida, was advertising that they were hiring. A few weeks later, I was on to the next chapter of this adventure called life.

Alfred E. Neuman of the famous *Mad Magazine* has stated, "Life is what happens to you while you are busy making other plans."

The Bible says, in Proverbs 19:21, "Many are the plans in a man's heart, but it is the Lord's purpose that prevails."

I have discovered that, when a job becomes a burden, stressful, and the enjoyment is sucked out of the work, this is the Lord saying, "Trust me. I have a better plan for you."

Chapter 6

SAILING IN NEW YORK

Water activities have always been an interest to our family. We started out with a canoe that was purchased through my brother, Richard, who had a marina and associated business in Lower Michigan. The canoe was purchased as a Christmas present to the family during our holiday visit with our families in upper Ohio, driving out from our home in Binghamton, NY. Our car was a station wagon with an installed roof rack. When it was time to return to New York, I turned the canoe right-side-up and secured it to the rack, and tied down front and back. I expected that the canoe could easily accommodate the Christmas presents and much of the luggage. Packing was difficult due to the shape of the canoe, and tying down a tarp was an even greater challenge. What I didn't fully appreciate was, because of the shape of the hull, when I was driving, the canoe tended to float up off the car. In addition, crosswinds and passing trucks would tend to cause the canoe to drift from side to side. There were very few places where I could securely tie to, and I ended up stopping many times to try different methods. Eventually we made it home without incident, but…live and learn.

I have always been convinced that the Lord likes us outside of our comfort zone, as that is where we see can see him the most. A comfort zone, in my mind, is a rut. Through the years since buying that canoe, we have gone many places with it, and still have it now fifty years later. Once, we were in the St. Lawrence River with Katie and me, along with three small kids and a dog. We just crept along the very edge of the river and were eventually stopped by the Coast Guard. They checked all of our life jackets and safety items and judged us legal, a bit overloaded, but okay. Memories…

As I write this chapter, I see that the Lord has been preparing us, little by little, for bigger adventures outside of our comfort zone. Not only have we enjoyed the journey, but he helps us build our confidence for even greater adventures where, again, we can experience his guidance. Fear of the unknown has not been mine to endure. Thank you, Lord!

We advanced from canoeing to sailing when a neighbor went off on an extended vacation and offered to loan us his sailboat. He had a fourteen-foot Starcraft on a trailer, a very stable boat to learn with. He showed me how to raise the mast in his backyard, and that was the extent of the checkout. I went to the library and loaned a book on the basics of sailing. The next Sunday afternoon had our first experience, sailing on a local lake. We had been planning a two-week trip to upper Michigan, so took the boat with us to Douglas Lake, where we had a family cottage. My brother, Lyle, also was there with his family, and we enjoyed the first week learning to maneuver and beach the boat. We were having so much fun we decided to take it to Mackinaw City, about twenty-five miles away, where the big bridge joined Lower Michigan with the Upper Peninsula. We decided to sail under the bridge and from there it looked like a short sail to Mackinaw Island. The sail only took about an hour to the island, and we docked at the marina in order to tour the town. After an hour or so, I started trying to get everyone back to the boat as I realized that we would be sailing into the wind and would take much longer to get back. Finally, we set off and, sure enough, the wind was exactly against us. It took us about four hours to get back, arriving after dark. Thus, thank you, Lord, we survived our first off-shore sail. Little could we have known that over forty years later, our very last sail would, unintentionally, bring us again through these same waters. How amazing, Lord!

Our sailing involvement then progressed to a used Sunfish. Our three older children were about ages eight, ten, and twelve. They were allowed to sail it alone after a checkout with Dad. The final test for each one of them was to tip the boat over and to right it by themselves, climb in, and sail away. This created much fun, but we needed another boat for the five of us.

Our Sunfish off the Long Island Sound
during the Bicentennial Celebration

On a Saturday in January in the Binghamton area, I took our youngest newborn, Bob, in my arms, who was six months old at the time, and drove to a small boating shop. I asked the owner if he had a fixer-up sailboat for a spring project. At first, he didn't think so and then remembered an old wooden-hull boat way back in the storage shed under a collection of stuff. For some reason, it had been painted three shades of green, and had a wooden mast and boom. It had a trailer, and was priced so I could afford it, and it was exactly what I was looking for; the make of it was called a Blue Jay.

Jim and our refurbished Blue Jay

Refurbishing it was a wonderful spring project, and I discovered that the Sunfish fit on top easily in order to trailer both boats at the same time. This wooden-hulled Blue Jay accommodated four people and was very stable in strong winds. In this way, the teens could have a variety of sailing experiences, and Katie and I could sail with our young son, Bob.

During my employment in Binghamton, NY, my income barely supported my four children and my stay-at-home wife. I was always exploring ways in which I could break away from my dependence on my employer, Singer-Link, due to the high stress of my job and extensive travel. One of the inspirations that I had was to develop a boat trailer that allowed the frame to be lowered to the ground. In this way, it would be easier to float a boat on and off during launch and recovery. I, somehow, was inspired to develop a design that would make this possible. What I discovered during this and many other engineering challenges since is that my early morning waking thoughts are my most productive times for design developments or for resolution of problems. I have learned that such inspiration comes from the Lord, as described in Psalm 139:17–18. I was convinced that there was a way, and I persisted and built a prototype for the Blue Jay. This design required less than six inches of water to float it on and off. I built this in our basement, and during this effort found that our thirteen-year-old son, Jim, had the visualization skills to help me with this project. From this experience, I could appreciate the talent that he had, and that ultimately resulted in his career as an architect. Jim also became my close sailing partner as we eventually learned to sail larger sailboats together. I have come to realize that much credit is due the Lord for such a plan that would significantly influence our lives for years to come.

I, ultimately, received a patent on this design and then proceeded to try to market it to trailer manufacturers. The manufacturers that I approached were favorable to this for small boats but wanted to see what could be done with larger ones that really presented a launching challenge. So, I proceeded to develop a larger version.

I was determined to build a model that would have such a higher capability, but I needed a boat for the design of another prototype. It just so "happened" that there was a boat show at Madison Square Garden in New Your City in February, and we all went as a family to the show. I really never expected to purchase a boat but needed one on which I could base my design. We found a delightful twenty-eight-foot Lancer sailboat that requiring only three feet of water to launch and recover. It was the largest boat that I could find and still be on a trailer. Perfect for my design! In discussions with the sales representative, he offered to sell the boat at one-third off the retail price, as he could see the potential for my unique design using their boat. As a result, we purchased a new one for delivery in May. The company had a manufacturing plant in nearby Connecticut, and this would give me enough time to build a trailer. The design was flexible enough that I thought that I could design and build it in Binghamton, and when the boat was ready for delivery, the trailer could be matched to the boat easily in Connecticut. Upon delivery, we pulled it to Ithaca, NY, that was near home, for sailing on Lake Cayuga—one of the Finger Lakes.

Local Firm to Produce Unique Trailer

Dean Bates, a local inventor from Sunrise Terrace, has ahosen a local company to produce his invention.
A new idea that Bates submitted to Innovative ssociates, of the industrial incubator in Johnson City, is a avolutionary design in boat trailers. Bates' boat trailer aoks a lot like any other boat trailer at first glance, but aere the similarity ends.
Bates has designed a trailer where the trailer bed can be awered to the ground level. This is accomplished by a aries of pulleys and a U-shaped axle.
In convenience terms this means bigger boats can be aunched in shallower water with fewer people needed to alp. This concept does not have to stop at boat use, a ailer with this special feature could be helpful in aowmobile, animal, or heavy machinery trailers.
The raising or lowering of the trailer bed is done through ae use of a hand winch. This hand winch is designed so aat one person can operate it easily.
Although these trailers could be 25 per cent to 30 per cent aore expensive than ordinary trailers, it could pay for self in time and convenience.
In a few weeks Bates will be going on a tour of boat shows ith his new trailer.

—M. Elizabeth Allen

Dean Bates' revolutionary boat trailer, from which boats can be lowered to ground level. (Photo by Tony Rossi, Jr.)

Prototype trailer for our new Lancer sailboat

We named the boat *Empathy*, a word that I was vaguely familiar with at the time. It is unbelievable that this name has become a hallmark description of how my life has developed through the years, in reaching out to and helping others. Thank you, Lord, for helping me decide on this name that would, eventually, be the one word describing my passion for helping others.

I made the modifications to the trailer and the redesign worked, but still needed perfecting. I believed that a trailer manufacturer could take this design and optimize it for production and utility. I, again, took it on the road to pursue an interested manufacturer, but found that the potential was not there. The economy was down (it was the 1970s), there was a severe gas shortage with prices very high, and this resulted in a down market for boats and trailers. To top it off, I discovered that trailer manufacturers were very conservative wanting to stay with their designs and were unwilling to invest in such a radical design. The timing was just not right, but we ended up with a beautiful boat that has allowed for innumerable, wonderful experiences to come.

Our beautiful Empathy

By this time, I had invested significantly by way of costs and time that I ceased all further activities. I have proceeded to use the trailer for our own boat needs for the past thirty-five years, allowing us to only launch the boat during the best season for sailing, and to store it at minimum or no cost. Thus, sailing has been much more affordable.

Within a few weeks of initial launch, Jim and I were out sailing together. The winds were very high and we were having a thrill using our largest sails so that the boat was heeled way over on its side. How exciting! When we approached the eastern shore and needed to "come about," I tried to turn the boat to bring the bow through the wind, the boat speed dropped off fast, and I lost control of the boat as it again headed toward shore. This was so perilous that a man came out of the cottage and ran out on his dock to watch us crash into the rocky shore. When I fully realized what was happening, I shouted for Jim to run forward and throw out the anchor. At the same time, I opened the lazaretto cover to get to the engine, but unfortunately the starter switch was loose and it had to be secured before the engine could start. When I finally got the motor going and into gear, the anchor caught turning the boat to bring the bow through the wind, and we joyfully sailed away from shore while I waived to the man on the dock. Thank you, thank you, Lord, for saving our beautiful new boat from such a pending disaster!

One of the driving forces that motivated me in sailing was that adrenalin rush that was very similar to what I had experienced with flying, except that I could now take the family on fun excursions. At this time, we had three teenagers. One of the additional justifications for purchasing *Empathy* was to have an adventure that would appeal to our kids, to keep us together as a family instead of them making other use of their time. They could bring a friend at any time, and we would accommodate them. This philosophy proved to be a good one, especially during the 1980s when our society became "anti-generational" and wanting to break away from parental relationships. Two of our sons have gone on to become sailors, and they own their own family-size boats. In retrospect, *Empathy* has proved to be affordable and allow for sailing adventures that were beyond our dreams at the time. This kept our family relationships close, and friendship memories that have endured. Only the Lord could have orchestrated a plan that has had such an impact on our lives and the lives of others in such a blessed way.

Stan was on the high school swim team as a diver, and he invited three of his friends from the team to go, along with our son, Jim, on a weekend bachelor cruise. What a wonderful experience it was, and we did the same for the next six years, as the boys proceeded through high school and then all went to different colleges. I personally enjoyed these bachelor cruises with just us guys. The conversations were very interesting, especially since they were all in different colleges. I would stay in the background and listen to the experiences that they were having individually—the stories and laughter that seemed never ending. Amazingly enough, the stories and language used was always clean and respectful. I must admit, however, that one warm afternoon when I was at the helm and they were all spread out taking a nap from staying up late the night before, I decided to bring them back to life. I called out in a loud voice "O my god, they're naked!" What a mad scramble ensued!

My son's friendships have all endured the test of time, and each of these friends has done very well in their education, employment, and in their marriages. One of them, Jim, came from a family that no one had ever graduated from high school, and lived in a low-income area of Binghamton. The close friendship that he developed with Stan and us encouraged him to not only graduate from high school but to go on to achieve a college degree. Upon graduation, Jim landed a job in New York City as an investment advisor for a prominent firm where he has excelled in his career. Only the Lord could have orchestrated and played a role in such an impact on all of these young men.

We sailed in Cayuga Lake for one season. The next summer, we decided to sail north into the Erie Canal, and from there across Lake Ontario to the St. Lawrence River.

During this trip, my mother and father came along from the beginning of the trip and through the Erie Canal. My father had the time of his life, as he was at the helm much of the time.

While we were sailing across Lake Ontario, we had very light winds and the kids wanted to go for a swim—in the middle of the lake and well away from shore. I was not a good swimmer and, as a young boy had developed a fear of swimming where I could not have the bottom near. I took down the sails to stop the boat, and the kids jumped in. I was never one to allow the kids to do something that I would not do, so I decided to jump in as well. Fear never came to me, as I realized that I would just swim on the surface, and who cares whether the bottom was ten feet below or a one thousand feet. Goodbye fear! The winds picked up later and we had a wonderful sail arriving at the town of Sackets Harbor in a sheltered marina at dusk. In less than one hour after we arrived, the winds picked up to an intensity that would have been overwhelming if we were still out sailing. Another huge "Thank you, Lord" for saving us from a situation that would have frightened us all significantly.

At the beginning of the St. Lawrence River was a section of the river approximately forty-five miles long that was referred to as the Thousand Islands. It actually contained over 1,800 miles and was a premier sailing area. We kept the boat at a marina directly across the river from these islands. At the end of my work day in Binghamton, Katie would have a picnic dinner that we would eat on the way, a three-hour trip. We would usually arrive in the dark, load the boat, and head across the river to anchor between two of the islands. It was always a thrill to wake up in the morning to see where we had arrived, and to enjoy the beauty of God's creation.

In the two years that we sailed this area I can clearly remember two specific incidences when the Lord saved us from a serious disaster. The charts were very detailed, but being human, we were prone to mistakes, and this was before the GPS. I really enjoyed night sailing as it somewhat gave me a similar adrenalin rush as during my flying days, navigating in the dark. During one of these night sails in a section of the river that was somewhat open, I knew that we were approaching a marker buoy but I had family members making it difficult to see straight ahead. Suddenly, I had the urge to reverse course and, as I did so, we passed right next to a buoy that was lighted and was very heavily built. If we had hit it, we surely would surly sunk the boat and, at night, this would have been disastrous. Another hundred "thank you, Lords" would have been appropriate.

Another time, as we were traveling between two islands that were rather close to each other, there was a marker between them. As I approached the marker, I thought that I knew on which side to take, so I was proceeding at a normal speed. As I approached the marker, I had a strong feeling that something was wrong, so I immediately reversed course at the very last minute. When I then checked the chart, I found that I was about to proceed directly upon a rock that was just below the surface of the water. This "strong feeling," I have now discovered, was the Holy Spirit helping me avoid a very serious collision. Thank you, Lord, from saving us from this impending disaster that would have sunk our beloved *Empathy*!

At the eastern end of the Thousand Islands lies an island with a hill on it that is about two hundred feet tall. At the very top of the hill is a very large cross marking the beginning of this beautiful waterway. As I write this book after over thirty-five years of sailing, virtually most of the east coast of the U.S., all around Florida, five trips to the Bahamas, and up the Intracoastal Waterway from Florida to Upper Michigan, I can say with conviction that the Thousand Islands area of God's world was the best of sailing that we have ever experienced. Thank you, Lord, for the opportunity of exploring your beautiful creation, and keeping us safe while doing so.

> All things bright and beautiful. All creatures great and small,
> All things wise and wonderful, the Lord God made them all.
> The cold wind in the wintertime, the pleasant summer sun,
> The ripe fruit in the garden time, He made them every one;
> He gave us eyes to see them all, and lips that we might tell
> How great is the Almighty God, who has made all things well.

> Text by Cecil F. Alexander, altered
> Music by Sunny Salsbury

> (I suggest that you Google "All Things Bright and Beautiful" and sung by the small children's choir, name unknown.)

Chapter 7

LIVING AND WORKING IN TAMPA, FLORIDA

After a total of eighteen years with Singer-Link in Binghamton, New York, I was delighted to move to beautiful Tampa, Florida, and to start again, this time with a small company of about 350 members. Katie, however, was devastated as she was leaving her church, friends, a classic Dutch Colonial home, and a nice neighborhood where our kids had grown up. It took two years before she would consider Tampa a permanent home. At this point, we were still not aware that the Lord was with us on a daily basis. Therefore, this chapter of my life was what I made of it while the Lord was making other plans. I would still not discover that the Lord was *personally* involved in our lives for another seven years.

Our beautiful home in Binghamton

One of my challenges during the relocation was bringing our boat, *Empathy*, to Florida. Stan had just graduated from the Air Force Academy and was home on leave before being activated in the Air Force. He volunteered to help me drive the boat to Florida with our big Mercury station wagon. Because we had two drivers, we decided to drive straight through. As we were on the Interstate going through the hills of Virginia, it started raining in the dark of the evening, and as I was driving, we came up over a hill and were directed over in the left single lane for construction ahead. As we topped the hill, suddenly there was a loud bang, the engine stopped, the electrical power went out, and the power steering and brakes were disabled. I yelled for Stan to get the flashlight out and shine it on the side of the road so that I could see where we were going. Down the hill we coasted and at the bottom was a bridge under repair, but on the other side of the bridge, the Interstate opened again to normal two-lane operation and we coasted to a stop on the shoulder where there was plenty of room to pull over. What a ride, and what a miracle! Saved by the grace of God! We climbed into the boat where we slept for the night, despite hearing truck after truck driving by.

In the morning, I determined that the alternator was the culprit and proceeded to take it off. We noted on the map that there was a two-lane road parallel to the Interstate just across the fence. The road led to a very small town a few miles away. This, of course, was still at a time before cell phones were available to help. We hitched a ride to this town and found a very small garage in operation. The sole mechanic did a check and confirmed that the alternator had failed, and he just happened to have a replacement in stock. He then offered to take us back to the car and helped get us underway. By noon this same day, we were on our way again. This was another clear example of your help, Lord, in time of need!

We then drove through the night, and early the next morning we needed gas. We got off the Interstate and drove to the nearest gas station to refuel. As we were getting into the car, we noticed that one of the trailer tires was completely shredded. The trailer had two axles and the other tires held up the boat without the driver being aware of a problem. The station operator suggested that we park across the road in a vacant lot while we resolved this dilemma. The tire was a very heavy-duty model, and I knew that it would be difficult to get a replacement on Sunday. As we were parking the boat, a pickup truck stopped alongside and the driver was just watching us. When I acknowledged him and went over to talk, he said that he was con-sidering purchasing a boat and was just admiring ours. He said that it was apparent that we were having tire trouble and wondered what size we needed. I told him, and he said the he had probably forty or fifty of them in his backyard, and that he would be glad to give me the best of the lot. It turns out that the size that I needed was a very common tire for mobile homes, not for cars, and he was in the busi-ness of transporting mobile homes. In his business, he would mount a set on the mobile home to be transported and take them off when he set up the home. We followed him to his house, picked out a tire, went to a garage that was open on Sunday to have it mounted. We were underway again by noon. Now, what is the chance that would happen without being a miracle? Money was a significant issue at that time, and to think that I got the tire for free! This event, Lord, was one of the clearest examples that I have ever had of your awareness of the details in my daily struggles, and solutions that you orchestrate in such a very unusual way to make it evident that it is from you. Thanking you, Lord, is hardly an adequate show of appreciation.

The next day after arriving in Tampa, I realized that I needed a place to store the boat. Considering that we were on the outer edge of our housing development, there were homes nearby that had vacant property next to them. I inquired at a house about a mile away, the people had a total of three acres, and they agreed to let me keep the boat there for free. How about that! Twenty-five years later, I was still able to use their property for storage, and the owner, Jack, passed away. His wife, Jeanine, needed maintenance help with her older house, which I have provided along with mowing her yard. Another huge blessing for both of us. Thank you, Lord!

My new business development position at Reflectone made use of much of my previous experiences: flight simulation training and technology, customer relations, sales, meeting customer support requirements, interfacing with company technical personnel, and coordination with management. I was able to develop a very unique way in which every one of the customer's specific requirements in their request for proposal (RFP) was answered and easily found in our proposal. In that way, we would receive a near-perfect score in their technical evaluation. The only other significant factor in winning the contract was the price. I had no direct input regarding the price, and this is where politics and management issues became pertinent. I had devised a way, however, for costs to be better identified and managed, and I presented this to management. This plan, however, became a "political football." I lost out and found myself not "playing the game." As a result, I spent six years struggling to win contracts and losing most of them over the price. I found myself in the first group to be "down-sized" when the company was sold off to British Aerospace. They decided that Reflectone would only build simulators to meet their needs and not to pursue other business opportunities. I was given forty-five minutes' notice to clean out my desk and process out.

Up until this time, I had always considered myself to be a "self-made" man who could make lemonade out of lemons, so to speak. I had always devised a solution out of all of the difficult circumstances that I had been through. Finally, the Lord gave me a problem that I couldn't solve—unemployment for eleven months. Throughout my adult life, I have always been convinced that the Bible's promises are true, and that the Lord would always supply my needs. I did not want to depend on the government for supplying my needs. In my prayers, I stated clearly that I was trusting the Lord to supply all my needs and, therefore, I did not apply for Unemployment Compensation.

By this time, I had nearly thirty years of experience in flight simulation, much of it with the airlines and a few other customers. I considered myself to be very well known and respected throughout the industry and getting another job would not be too difficult. As it turned out, the simulation market was not growing, it was a mature market with significant competition, and the economy was down. I was fifty-five years old and age was definitely against me. Although I had a respectable background in management, I was unable to change career fields, as I needed to know the products where I applied for work.

Since the time that we were married, Katie and I were members of and active in the Episcopal churches. About six months into my unemployment I had a very strong feeling that I was missing something spiritually and decided that I would change churches. I noticed a sign pointing to a new Methodist Church nearby, and one Sunday Bob and I decided to attend. After the service as we walked out of the church, I looked at Bob and said, "What do you think?"

He responded, "I think we have found a new home, Dad."

There was something about the feeling of the service and the warmth of the people that spiritually touched us. About a month later, Katie agreed to join us, and our lives were subsequently changed forever.

I have also come to comprehend the true meaning of friendship. Of all of the innumerable "friends" that I made during the twenty-five years in simulation, including six years at Reflectone, not one of them ever contacted me at any time to see how I was doing during my unemployment. I have, therefore, become convinced of how few people that we consider as friends are willing to stick with you through the struggles of life. This realization has served me well in the years to come, as I reach out in my personal ministry to others during their times of need. When I come along the side of someone hurting, I stay along their side beyond the better times that come—I try to be a friend forever.

As I looked back at my thirty-one years in corporate life, I have learned many important lessons. The bottom line of it all is that if you work at it with all your heart, as working for the Lord (Col. 3:23) the Lord will reward you, and may be telling you that he has a better plan for you. I had always approached my corporate life with a full commitment to accomplishing all of my responsibilities well. I had devoted literally thousands of unpaid overtime hours, with integrity as my goal. And yet, I was given forty-five minutes to terminate my employment. Although it was dramatic at the time, my following the Lord's leadership has brought me a beautiful life of joy and all the other fruits of the Spirit (Gal. 5:22).

I have also come to realize that through these many years of struggle, we had as a family and as a marriage a collection of memories and experiences that bless us immeasurably. Truly, the strength to endure in a positive way came from the deep love that Katie and I have always had for each other, and the encouragement and conviction that the Lord will provide.

> Sometimes in the morning when shadows are
>   deep,
> I lie here beside you just watching you sleep.
> And sometimes I whisper what I'm thinking of
> My cup runneth over with love.

Sometimes in the evening when you do not see
I study the small things you do constantly,
I memorize moments that I'm fondest of,
My cup runneth over with love.

In only a moment we both will be old
We won't even notice the world turning cold,
And so, in these moments with sunlight above,
My cup runneth over with love.

Songwriters: Harvey
Schmidt and Tom Jones
Lyrics: Warner/Chappel

(I suggest that you Google "My Cup Runneth Over" sung by Ed Ames.)

Chapter 8

SAILING IN FLORIDA

After settling in Tampa, we were attracted to Tarpon Springs and a delightful marina on the Anclote River that leads directly into the Gulf of Mexico. One time, we were sailing with Tommy, a twelve-year-old boy from next door. We proceeded to anchor the boat at the end of the Anclote Island. As I set the anchor, I came to realize that the boat was not heading into the wind, for some reason. Just then I came to understand that there was a strong current from the outgoing tide that dominated the boat's direction. At that very time, Tommy jumped into the water and began to rapidly be taken out by the current toward the Gulf of Mexico. I immediately jumped in to save him, although I was not a strong swimmer. Katie had the foresight to rapidly release the inflatable dinghy that drifted along with us. We were able to swim over to the dinghy, climb in, and work our way back to the boat. It was only by the grace of God that we had the dinghy with us, that Katie was led to release it, and that we were able to swim to it before we were exhausted and taken out to sea.

Another time, after a strong storm had passed the previous day, Bob and I decided to sail out to Anclote Island to see if we could find some interesting sea shells. On the way back, we were confronted with a serious thunderstorm while in the river. We had no choice but to ride out the storm, and we set two anchors in the river. After the storm subsided, we realized that we had been blown into shallow water but afloat, and that a large power boat nearby was on the shore. As we accessed our dilemma, a man came out on a dock nearby and mentioned that, if we were able to work our way nearer his dock near shore, he explained that there was a channel dredged out that would take us back to the river. We were then able to do so and could return to the marina without further difficulty. O Lord, how can we thank you enough for keeping us and the boat safe, and that we were able to work our way out of the shallow water.

Hurricane season in Florida officially starts in June but is not usually active until August and later. These storms usually begin off the coast of Africa with lots of warning for the Tampa area. Rarely do hurricanes build up in the Gulf of Mexico and have rarely, if ever, developed in the upper Gulf of Mexico and come backward into the Tarpon Springs/Anclote area. In May of 1993, Bob and three of his friends wanted to take the boat out for a weekend cruise, beginning late afternoon on Friday. Bob was eighteen years old at the time and was practically raised on the boat. As they were about to head over from Tampa in the early afternoon, the TV reported that there was a storm in the Gulf of Mexico northwest of the Anclote area. I advised Bob to stay on the National Weather Radio (NOAA) on the VHS radio that we had, and not to go out if the weather got bad. As we watched the TV reports, it became apparent that the storm was backing down into the Anclote area where Bob was, but we never believed that it would continue backward. I assumed that Bob was listening to the VHF marine weather advisory and would be staying in the marina and not venture out. We just surmised that the updated TV weather that we were seeing was also available to boaters through the marine radio advisory. This was in the days before cell phones, and there was no way we could get in touch with them directly.

We never had a concern for them as we were convinced that they were safe in the marina. The next morning at 7:30 we received a call from Bob saying, "Guess where we are, Dad." He was calling on the Coast Guard marine radio, and he was calling from an island just off the Anclote River, and that they were okay. The two anchors were holding although the high waves were breaking over the island and it was very rough for them. We, again, received a call from him about eleven o'clock reporting that they were still hanging on. The next call came at 4:30 telling us that they had been blown ashore and were okay. Would we please come and get them in Palm Harbor.

As it turned out, one of the anchor lines had chaffed through and broke, and the one remaining anchor could not keep them in place. As they were drifting toward shore, they started up the motor that, in the severe pitching of the boat, ripped the fiberglass off the stern that was holding it, and the motor went bye-bye. Then they tried using just a little jib sail, and this soon shredded. As they were drifting toward shore over a shallow area, they called the Coast Guard who advised them that there was no way that they could come get them and, since there was not a threat to life, to ride it out to shore. Eventually, they drifted up to a sea wall and stepped ashore, and there was a dock that was ahead of them about fifty feet away. They pulled the boat to the dock where they secured it. All of them went down inside the boat and prayed together to thank the Lord for saving them from the storm.

Early the next week, we borrowed another motor and the owner of the property described that there was a channel dredged out such that we could maneuver the boat through the shallow waters. Besides the loss of the motor and one anchor, the sail that could be repaired, and a little fiberglass damage, all was well. The Lord doesn't promise to keep us from our storms of life but, instead, to be with us *through* our storms.

It turned out that the storm had built up so fast that it was never officially named as a hurricane or tropical storm. As a result, this storm has always been referred to as the No Named Storm. There were a total of eleven lives that were lost at sea in that area of the Gulf of Mexico, mostly commercial fishermen that were caught out. Also, a sailboat had drifted past Bob's area and was carried under a small bridge. As it drifted under the bridge, the boat capsized and three people lost their lives.

Thank you, Lord, for the safety of Bob and his crew, and resulted in only minimum damage to our dear *Empathy*!

As we approached one of the Christmas holidays, we were not planning to travel to Ohio to be with family and we had none in the area. So, I proposed that we put the boat in the water in Tampa Bay and sail to Key West. We had a friend, Jim Wilson, who was living there for the winter, and we then planned to spend Christmas Eve and Day with him. Katie, Bob, and I set off late on Tuesday before Christmas was on Saturday. We had all of the winds that we would want from the north, directly behind us, and very cool! We sailed all that day, all night, and got to the beginning of Charlotte Harbor, to a marina that afternoon. We stayed overnight at the marina and met Bob's friend, Lynn, who brought warmer clothes for us and joined us for the rest of the trip. We launched again the next morning, Thursday, sailing again in very heavy, cool winds from the north. We sailed all that day, all night, and the next afternoon arrived at Key West—Christmas Eve. We met Jim and went to a very nice friend's home for a wonderful dinner party, and then to Christmas Eve service at a beautiful Episcopal Church. The next day, Christmas Day, we toured the town and had dinner with Jim.

Early Sunday morning, I went by myself to a nine o'clock church service at a church near the marina, while the others slept in. I arrived about fifteen minutes early and leafed through a hymnal to look at the many hymns that address storms. I reflected on the fact that all of our early family pioneers had to have come by boat, and many had, without a doubt, experienced storms. I also felt a very long way from Tampa Bay, after four days and two nights with the best of following winds. I also realized that we would probably have to beat our way against the wind, and how long would that take us? After the service I returned to the boat, and by that time the rest of the crew had gotten their act together. As I sat down, I turned the radio on to the weather channel. The forecast *immediately* reported that the winds were expected to swing around to the southeast that afternoon and be strong. I immediately announce that we were launching as soon as possible, as these winds were perfect for starting out. As it turned out, we could set sail with winds from behind and could sail directly to Charlotte Harbor without having to adjust the sails. Again, we sailed all that day, that night, and the next afternoon arrived at our friend's dock on a canal in North Ft. Meyers. We had made arrangements with our friend, Bob Hemmenway, to stay overnight and to dock *Empathy*. We all returned to Tampa for the week, and Bob and Lynn came back the next weekend to bring the boat back to Tampa Bay. Thank you, Lord, for safety of our very first off-shore, long-distance trip, with *perfect winds* the entire voyage!

From the Key West trip, we were then inspired to sail off the Florida east coast to the Bahamas Islands that are as close as fifty miles. In the years to come, we made four ten-day trips, trailering the boat to Ft. Lauderdale on Friday, launching it and putting up the mast on Saturday, and heading out that evening for an overnight sail. During the first attempt, the winds were too high to put up the mast for several days, so we cancelled the trip and sailed locally for the few remaining days after the winds died down. One of those days, we decided to motor down the Intracoastal Waterway until later that afternoon when we punch out into the Gulf Stream. We then sailed back in the late afternoon and evening to Ft. Lauderdale. As we were heading back, a thunderstorm loomed directly ahead about ten miles, which would take us probable two hours to get to it. Being in the Gulf Stream, we could only get protected by entering an inlet to the Waterway. But we decided to press on and en route, we observed the storm dissipate before our eyes. By the time that we got to our inlet, it was dark. The inlet was marked by lighted buoys, but the problem was that the lights were nearly impossible to pick out due to the multitude of lights from homes along the coast. As we were contemplating our dilemma, along came a cruise ship returning from the Bahamas. It was perfect timing for us to follow it into the inlet. Thank you, Lord, for protection from the storm and for showing us the way to safety ashore.

The next week, Katie had to return to Tampa to teach in our church day-school. So without her, Bob, his friend Lynn, and I took the first trip to the town of West End on the Grand Bahama Island. There was a marina in the town, and this was the nearest point of land to Florida. In subsequent years, we made two trips to Freeport and its vicinity. One year, we went to Bimini Island that was off from Miami, with Katie, Bob, and Lynn. Katie and I decided to check into a motel at the marina while the guys went out to an adjacent island to anchor overnight by themselves. That evening, a storm hit during the early hours of the evening, after dark. When the boys came back the next day, they announced that a storm had hit them, with winds directly into the nice bay where they were anchored with two other boats. One of the other boats was a thirty-six-foot sailboat that was being ferried by a certified captain. They said that our boat, *Empathy*, weathered the storm well, but the other sailboat was blown ashore and was on its side. Also, *Empathy*'s two anchor lines were twisted such to indicate that they had rotated twice around, evidencing the possibility of near-tornado winds. Thank you, Lord, for saving all lives and for holding *Empathy* fast, with no damage!

After another of these trips, I was trailering the boat alone back across Alligator Alley (Interstate 75) and was experiencing headwinds that slowed my progress considerably. As I approached the west coast of Florida where I-75 turns from west to north, I heard a weather forecast that announced that the winds were turning from west to north, thus, having me experience continuing headwinds. When I heard this, I responded out loud, "Lord, what is it? It seems that we had headwinds nearly the entire trip." Immediately after thinking this, these exact words came to me: "If you would have dwelt on the headwinds, you would have missed the joy of the journey!" There was no doubt that this came from the Lord speaking to me as clear as if he was sitting next to me. And what a great lesson in life—if we dwell on the headwinds of life, we will miss the joy of the journey. How very true!

The fifth trip to the Bahamas was just Katie and I. I had re-engineered the boat for longer cruising, installing a portable generator to charge two deep-cycle batteries for powering an apartment-size refrigerator that I installed along with a toaster oven, and a two-burner alcohol stove. The outside of the boat was entirely painted, and a roller-reefing system was installed in order to roll the jib in and out without going forward. After sailing the boat for twenty-five years manually attaching the jib, the roller-reefing was so nice that I would often remark that I liked it so well I might marry it. After a while, Katie made the comment that she was concerned that I might divorce her and marry the roller-reefing system.

This final trip to the Bahamas turned out to be seven weeks long. We started out in Tampa Bay, sailed the Gulf of Mexico down to entrance to Charlotte Bay where we again stayed in the same marina as the Key West visit. We had planned on sailing around the lower part of Florida and then head out to the Bahamas. A large, old two-masted schooner was docked next to us. As we talked, the other captain informed us that we could shave many days off out trip by traversing up Charlotte Bay and into the river that comes from Lake Okeechobee. At the lake, a canal has been constructed around it such that there was plenty of depth and from there around the south end of the lake, and through a channel east to the Intracoastal Waterway leading out to the Gulf Stream toward the Bahamas. He said that he had just come that way and had all of the charts that we could have, as he would never use them again. This saved us nearly a week of heavy travel, and it turned out to be a very pleasant trip. Thank you, Lord, for your attention to the details of this adventure, including providing us with free charts.

The voyage around the Grand Bahama Island was a pure delight. Bob flew out in a very small charter plane to Freeport. We picked him up at the airport with a rented motor scooter, and he was with us for the next week as we proceeded to Hope Town, where he flew out of back to the U.S.

On the eastern side of the Grand Bahamas are the Abaco Islands. As we were traversing these islands, we learned that a hurricane had developed in the Gulf of Mexico, some five hundred miles away. The weather radio advised that winds in the Bahamas could be significant from this hurricane, and to take shelter. We found a very good anchorage in a nice sheltered bay. Even though the storm system was that far away, we had serious enough winds while we were anchored very near to the marina, the winds were such that we dare not row our dingy to the marina. For that reason, so we stayed on board for the entire day. Thank you, Lord, that you provided a safe shelter for us. The hurricane convinced us that we were pressing the season. The Bahamas gets hit nearly every year; therefore, it was time to head home to Florida.

The trip back across the Gulf Stream was expected to take all day, from dawn to dusk. We found a very small island off the northwest corner of the Grand Bahama Island, appropriately called

Memory Rock. This island turned out to be just a very large rock with nothing growing on it, and it only had a navigation beacon. There was not a bit of land anywhere in sight, and no sheltered bay in which to anchor for the night and feel secure. It was a very weird feeling, but we had no choice, so we tucked in close to the leeward side. We decided to wake up at the crack of dawn to get underway as soon as possible. When we woke up and looked out, we observed two thunderstorms that were nearby; one to the northeast that was no threat to us, and one to the west between us and the coast of Florida. We were not about to head into the later one, and Katie suggested that we go below and pray about it—whether to go or stay. After the prayer, we again came up and observed that the Florida one was dissipating before our eyes and it was replaced by a *rainbow* from the sun that was coming up from the east. That was clearly an answer to our prayer and a thrill to even think of today. What a spectacular answer to our prayer, Lord, and we had no doubt that this was a "go" from you.

There were no clouds and no winds on our return trip, so we ended up motoring all the way. It was a very warm day, in July, and to cool off Katie and I would take turns scooping up dumping a pail of water on each other. About two o'clock in the afternoon, as the trip was slowly proceeding with no land in sight, suddenly a large pod of dolphins surrounded our boat. We estimated about thirty of them, some jumping out of the water, some passing along side and across the bow, large ones and babies. What a show that went on for nearly thirty minutes, and suddenly they disappeared. In all of our sailing days, we had never experienced such a sight. Thank you again, Lord, for such a beautiful show!

After a totally calm trip, we approached the inlet into the Intracoastal Waterway. Just inside the waterway was a nice bay to anchor for the night. Suddenly, and without warning, we entered very turbulent waters! We were tossed around violently until we got into the waterway, where it was calm again. This was a very frightening experience as it was so unexpected. We found our anchorage just as it was getting dark after sundown. What a day from beginning to the end! The timing was perfect to allow for a daylight passage, and if it had been dark when we hit the turbulence, it would have been an even more dangerous experience. Thank you, Lord, for a safe passage and where your presence was so very apparent, and thank you for the surprising, beautiful experience with the dolphins!

Lyrics of this song come to mind:

> I pray you'll be our eyes, and watch us where we go
> And help us to be wise in times when we don't know
> Let this be our prayer, when we lose our way
> Lead us to a place, guide us with your grace
> To a place where we'll be safe.
>
> I pray we'll find your light,
> And hold it in our hearts
> When stars go out each night.
> Remind us where you are.
>
> Let this be our prayer
> When shadows fill our day
> Guide us with your grace
> Give us faith so we'll be safe.
>
> —"The Prayer" by David W. Foster,
> Tony, Carole Bayer Sager, and Alberta Test

The thrills from our sailing adventures and the confidence that we gained propelled us to consider the next sailing chapters in our lives—sailing up the Intracoastal Waterway to Upper Michigan.

Chapter 9

SPIRITUAL AWAKING

When I was growing up, I always had a spirit of love, cooperation, and joy being with my relatives, teachers, and friends. Although I was born in the middle of the Great Depression, no one had more fun in life than I did. I enjoyed all the activities in the church and liked to sing with my father in the semi-annual county Methodist Rally, when there was a men's choir. I believe that, from a young age, I always had an open heart for the Lord. I was always interested in participating in the summer vacation Bible school (VBS) at the Methodist Church, and then joined the Nazarene Church's VBS for another week. During these activities, one of the challenges presented was to learn the names of all sixty-six books of the Bible. To this day, I can recite most of them in order, although I could now use some practice. When I was about twelve years old, I participated in a three-day Christian youth camp about one hundred miles away from home. I was thrilled to be on my own, and I can still remember one of the unique songs that we learned and sang at the end of our meals. When I was about fourteen, I was able to go to the six-day Lakeside Retreat Center on Lake Erie. This was really a big deal as I was with high school kids. During the Friday evening service, I accepted the invitation to go forward to the altar, and to pray for Jesus to come into my heart and my life. Unfortunately, for the next forty years of faithful church attendance, I was never made aware of what this offered to me in my daily struggles in life. I went on to do my best in all of my endeavors and experiences without being aware that I had help with me 24-7. It is only now that I can see that the Lord was faithfully answering my needs and prayers, all along, and saving me from disasters, filling my needs even though I was not aware and grateful at the time.

After a total of ten months of unemployment, our Methodist Church Men's Group participated in a retreat at Leesburg, FL, and I was invited to attend. At that time, I knew no one in the group. During the Friday night group discussions, I shared my dilemma of unemployment. At Saturday lunch, a man who I had not previously met, pulled up a chair at the end of the table by me, and we discussed our mutual income dilemmas for the next two hours. He introduced himself as Ernie, and I found out that he too was desperate for income. He had moved down from Ohio a year prior and was struggling to establish a real estate business. In our discussions Ernie was clearly well established in his faith, and shared that Christ was alive, was aware of our needs, and would meet them in his time and way. Ernie asked me whether I had specifically invited Jesus into my heart and life. I responded that I had, but I was an engineer and if I couldn't figure it out and make sense, how could I believe it? Ernie responded that I can't possibly know the mind and power of God, but that I just needed to "give it up to him" and he will show that he is part of my circumstances. At the evening service, I went forward to the altar. Ernie followed me up and prayed with me and for me. I definitely was spiritually touched at that time.

About a week later on a Friday morning when nothing was happening at home, in desperation I knelt on my knees—for the first time—in my living room and pleaded for help from the Lord. Less than two hours later, I received a call from the son of an owner of a company in Michigan, who I had done a little business with several years before. He was on vacation in Orlando and was coming through Tampa the next day on his way to Clearwater. He called to invite me to lunch at which time I shared my circumstances. He indicated that they certainly could use me in the company to expand their business into flight simulation. Their company, St. Lawrence, refurbishes hydraulic equipment, and the flight simulators utilize hydraulics in the motion and flight control systems. Ten days later, I was in Michigan to sign an employee agreement with St. Lawrence—a company that I had not been in touch with for several years. This employment was *clearly* an answer to my prayer, and I was convinced at that time that the Lord was the real deal! I became certain that he was with me 24-7 and that he had plans for me. I was able to stay in Tampa and establish an office in my home. My territory was the entire simulator market, airline and military worldwide. I was subsidized for the first year, and then I was on my own financially to live on commissions.

As I am writing this story, a song came to mind that I was vaguely familiar with and had to call my buddy Ernie to help me fine the title of the song so that I could look it up on the Internet. It turned out to be "I Don't Need to Understand, I Just Need to Hold His Hand":

> Life is like a mighty sea, so tossed and driven,
> Billows rise through the hearts of every man.
> Storms so many times would leave the heart with
> questions.
> You don't need to understand, you just need to
> hold his hand.
>
> I don't need to understand, I just need to hold
> his hand.
> I don't need to ask the reason why.
> For I know he'll make a way, through the night
> and through the day
> I don't need to understand, I just need to hold
> his hand.
>
> One day my life down here will be through, and
> he will call me to my
> Home over there on that golden shore.
> I'll look back, review the path that lay before me.
> I won't care to understand anymore.

I don't need to understand, I just need to hold
    his hand
I won't ever need to ask the reason why,
For I know he'll make a way, through the night
    and through the day,
I don't need to understand, I just need to hold
    his hand.

—Magdalene Crocker

(I suggest Google the title and listen to
Jimmy Swiggart.)

One of the first things that I experienced after my conviction was that I had a thirst to read and learn what was in the Bible. Although I had several Bibles in the house, never had I ever even opened the cover to study scripture. My impression was that I had a hard time reading the Bible in the past as it was the King James Version filled with "thees" and "thous," which turned me off. One of the books that I found in my library was a New International Version that was revised with much easier-to-understand language. This book had been given to us by a distant relative, inscribed and dated ten years prior. I had never even cracked the cover and didn't even remember that it had been given to us. This version spoke to me from day one. I didn't know anything about the Bible except that there was an Old Testament and a New Testament, and I could name the sixty-six books in their order. Because I did not know anything about the Bible and wanted to more quickly get a feel for it, I took five yellow sticky notes for bookmarks and placed them in different places throughout. I placed one in Genesis, Psalms, Proverbs, Mathew, and Ephesians, and each day I would read at least one chapter from each. I was amazed that almost every day a scripture would be so meaningful to me that I wanted to be able to find it again. I would, therefore, make a note of them on the yellow bookmarks. When the bookmarks were filled up, I would set them aside and get a new one. Finally, they added up to the point that I typed them up in the computer, making my own index. I remember that I began with a title for the index "Dean's 55 Favorite Scriptures." I soon ran well beyond fifty-five and it has developed into an eleven-page document, single spaced. Unfortunately, this index was typed into a laptop computer that has long since gone away along with the program.

Favorite Scripture References

As a result, the attached illustration of it today has additional references handwritten all over it. It has been a wonderful source of inspiration during my many years since—especially helpful in my outreach to others. Where did this thirst come from? The answer can only be from my renewed spirit from the Lord, beginning at age fifty-five, when I realized that he lives with me at all times. What an amazing realization! Along with it came a profound change in my spiritual craving for more and more of what the Lord wants to say to me, and to do with me.

> O soul, are you weary and troubled?
> No light in the darkness you see?
> There's light for a look at the Savior,
> And life more abundant and free!
>
> Turn your eyes upon Jesus,
> Look full in His wonderful face,
> And the things of earth will grow strangely dim,
> In the light of His glory and grace.
>
> —Helen Howarth Lemmel
>
> (Treat yourself by going to Google, type in "Turn Your Eyes Upon Jesus," and listed to Alan Jackson's song.)

Another strong urge that I had was to listen to Christian radio, especially Moody Radio, through the local radio station WKES. Their programming was essentially a variety program of news, music (the old traditional hymns), Bible teachers such as Chuck Swindal, speakers such as through Focus on the Family, news, and commentary on current events. I often would record programs that I would like to refer to again. These recordings became a great source of inspiration, as I would play them over during the many road trips that I would take later in promoting the business.

During the time that I had the office in my home, Katie's mother, Helen, came to live with us full time. She was ninety-five years old and had virtually lived out of a suitcase for the previous thirty years. Katie's father had died at age fifty-three and Helen became a house mother in a men's dormitory at the University of Michigan where she resided until retirement at age sixty-five. Then, for the next thirty years, she lived out of a suitcase while visiting her four children, each for three to four months before moving on to the next one. She felt blessed that she could maintain close contact with her children and become personally involved in her grandchildren. Katie and Florida appealed to her, so our home welcomed her permanently for the remainder of her days. We had three bedrooms but they are all on the second floor, which was too much for her to navigate. Therefore, we moved our dining room table and chairs to the side and established a bedroom for her on the first floor so that she did not have to go up the stairs except for a shower. We had a half-bathroom on the first floor, but it was down three steps. This arrangement worked very well at first, except that she was lonely during the day as Katie was teaching a pre-kindergarten class in our Church Day School, and I had a business to develop upstairs.

Whenever we were home, Mom would beg us to come and sit with her for a while. When I was not traveling and was in my office, I would always have a radio on in the background, tuned to the Moody Radio Christian station. This helped me to grow spiritually, better understanding of what my new life with the Lord was really all about. I was, thereby, greatly fulfilled and inspired. My thought was what a help it would be if only Katie's mother could listen to it as well. At her age, however, it would be difficult for her to manage a radio. I then devised a way to splice in a large volume control into the speaker system of a radio and mounted it remotely on a bean bag that would be on the nightstand next to her bed. The radio was placed under her bed, always tuned to WKES. In this way, she was able to wake up in the morning and while still lying in bed could turn up the volume and listen to it as she wanted at any time. She really took to it and was never as lonely as before. She loved to listen to the music while going to sleep, in the middle of the night, or anytime she wanted it, and still be able to turn the volume off at will. She had been a lifetime member of the Episcopal faith, and this evangelical radio station programming was new and appealed to her. A few months later, I overheard a telephone conversation that she had with her son in California, and she mentioned that she wanted him to know that she was now "a real Christian." It was her way of telling him that she now had Jesus into her life. Hallelujah! And what a difference this made in her outlook on life.

The tapes that I made of the Moody programs turned out to be very helpful to me. As I would travel out by car to promote the business, I would have these wonderful resources to listen to. My desire was to dedicate each trip to the Lord, to protect my travels and guide me along the way. To do so, I would have a juice-only fast for the first day of the trip and for the last day of return. Each of these days, I would listen to only a local Christian radio station, to Christian music, or listen to the WKES tapes. In this way, I learned to walk with the Lord 24-7, a perspective that I still try to live with each day, in every way. I was thereby inspired all the time, I was gaining new insight into my faith, and it made the many miles go by with ease.

I learned that, as I would try to set up appointments along the way, if I tried to contact a key client and for some reason and I failed to be able to with contact him after two tries, I would take this as a "no" from the Lord and move on. Very often, I would later learn that it would have been a waste of time and was better to move on to other clients. As a result of this sales experience, I became totally at ease with meeting new people. I would just let the conversation flow naturally instead of a canned marketing pitch. This experience has served me well in my later years that, during my ministry of others, I would let my discussions flow with thoughts that I am convinced were inspired. This was clearly demonstrated with a dying friend, Peggy, during what would be the last time we would see her before she died of cancer. At this time, my good friend, Ernie, was our Sunday school class teacher. I felt led to invite the class to meet with Peggy, but what an awkward visit this would be. As we greeted Peggy, I was led to suggest that we sing some hymns, and everyone enjoyed joining in. Between hymns, Ernie and I started telling stories about funny events in our lives, from which we gleaned many laughs. Peggy really enjoyed this time together. What a joyful event it turned out for everyone! I have really learned that if we involve the Lord in our events, the thoughts and words are not solely our own. He wants to speak through us, and at the same time to take away our anxieties over what to say. Thank you, Lord, for how you inspire us when we need it.

As I mentioned before, my brother, Neil, had learning disabilities apparently from experiencing polio as an infant. As he was growing up, we never expected him to be able to drive, hold a job, or, especially, get married. The Lord, however, had other plans, as each of these challenges, in time, were overcome. Until he was about forty-five years, he had been living with our parents and they were greatly concerned about how he would be taken care of when they were gone. At that time, a woman, Ila, came into his life and they were married a year later. She had come from a troubled background and previous marriage, but was attracted to Neil and to our family. A few months after they were married, I was in the Detroit area on business, for one week each month. Detroit was only about two hours from Fayette, and I was able to visit my families much more often than I ever had for forty years. During one of these visits Mom and I were talking to Ila and sharing how valuable it was for us to attend church. Suddenly, Ila got up and stormed out of the house. A short time later, I went to their house to apologize to her if we had offended her. In tears, she explained that she didn't feel worthy of being in our family due to her previous troubled years. I explained to her that God loves us all equally, and upon our invitation he wants to come into our life and to help us through our troubled times. I stated that Mom and I would never again pressure her to come to church and that she should just "watch me." I don't know where that thought came from, but it certainly didn't come from me. Soon thereafter, Ila started attending church with Neil, as he was a regular attender. A few months later, I was in Detroit when my mother died, and I was there for her funeral. It was at this time that Katie's mother had come to Tampa to live with us, and the need for my monthly trips to Detroit just happened to be concluded. I could then spend more time with Katie's mother. As time went by, Ila said that she had been watching me, as I suggested, and recognized how the Lord seemed to have me at the right time at the right place. As a result, she was attending church with Neil on a regular basis. In the years to come, she demonstrated her faith and trust in the Lord, and greatly attributed it to watching me. Thank you, Lord, for using me as a living testimony in such an unusual way.

Katie's mother and I always had a special mother-to-son relationship. She did, however, tend to have negative tendencies. Also, as is common in people as they advanced in age, upon impulse she might say something that I knew that she didn't really mean. I found that when this would occur, I could just go to her, give her a big hug, and she would melt on the spot, as if to say that she was sorry, but she would never say it. I had to classify her as basically a pessimist. When she was in the hospital in what turned out to be her last twenty-four hours, I was in her hospital room when the doctor came in. He said that the results of his analysis were that she had a blockage in the intestines, and the only way that it could be eliminated was through surgery. He needed her permission, of course, to which she responded: "That's okay, Doc. You gotta do what you gotta do." The operation was then scheduled for the next morning. The rest of the day and evening, her attitude was up and positive. As Katie and I left the hospital that evening, I remarked to Katie that this was the first day ever that I could consider her mother to be an optimist. The next day, her mother never recovered from the surgery as her blood pressure dropped, and it never came back. The Lord took her painlessly and peacefully. I knew that being positive the last day of her life this was God's way of demonstrating that she was in his care. Thank you, Lord, for such a clear way of showing that this was part of your plan for her life, at age ninety-eight.

Less than a year later, Katie's brother-in-law, Cal Canfield, was near the end of a nine-year battle with Parkinson's disease and dementia. I was in the area on business, so dropped in for an overnight visit. Cal had not been able to express a thought for well over a year. When I was ready to leave, I hugged him and said, "Goodbye, Cal. I love you."

To which he responded, "I love you too, Dean."

About a month later, he died. Thank you, Lord, for such an amazing way of demonstrating that you were involved by helping Cal acknowledge and respond to my expression of love to him.

Our son, Jim, and his family were living in Rhode Island. He was a licensed architect and found an opportunity in Gaylord, Michigan, beginning in the first part of November. Gaylord is a town of about 3,500 people. His wife, Kim, and son Spencer stayed in RI until the house was sold. They lived in a very desirable neighborhood and they expected their home to sell easily. About three weeks later on Sunday before Thanksgiving, I talked with Kim who was crying and very discouraged, as the house had been shown to a number of people but no one had made an offer. As we concluded the discussion, I asked if she would like to pray about it and we did. After the prayer, I was encouraged to say that I believed that the Lord would show that he was involved, and there would be evidence of this within one week. We did not talk again until Friday, five days later, when she told me that Monday they received two offers. Tuesday the realtor went to each of them to submit their best-and-final offer. On Wednesday, they received the winning offer, and it was more than the asking price. Not only that, but these people were from Gaylord, Michigan. What an absolutely amazing demonstration of your answer, Lord, to our prayer!

Along with my musical interests most of my life, I have always taken a liking to the great hymns of the past. Early in my new awareness of my personal walk with the Lord, I woke up to the fact that every morning early after arising, there was a hymn being played in the background of my mind. And, the hymn would change every day. I was so intrigued that I started writing the titles on scraps of paper that I accumulated as time went by. When I had accumulated over twenty-five of them, I stopped writing them down. This phenomenon has continued to this day, and it is usually a hymn, but occasionally a popular song of the past. Where does this come from? Certainly not of my thinking. The only thing that I can attribute it to is the Holy Spirit is demonstrating to me that he is present.

One day, at age seventy, I sat down at the piano at home, and suddenly a chord came to me that sounded good, and I was soon able to play a hymn "by ear." I really liked the sound of it, and for the next eight years, I would play any hymn that came to mind, pulling out dozens of hymns of the past. I have been so inspired that I still play nearly every day, and I have given up struggling with printed music. A few years ago, a very good widowed Christian friend checked into a nearby senior-living home. The first Sunday that she was there, Katie and I visited her. In our discussions, she mentioned that they could really use some more music at this home. I took this as a calling from the Lord to share my newfound talent at the piano with others. I offered to provide a sing-along activity each month, which we did for nearly two years, until I lost my musical partner, Katie. The residents asked to have the words to the hymns provided so that they could sing along with the music. As a result, I typed out song sheets with two verses for each of approximately fifteen hymns, with Katie leading and helping them find the right page and lyrics. The most amazing thing is that I have obtained books of the popular songs of the '40s, and I have added my versions of the songs of this era that we all loved when we were young. This has become well received and, after all of these years, I am now playing what I desired to play in the "good ole days." I never cease to be amazed at how my fingers are directed to the right keys. I never memorize a song, and I play it as the Spirit leads me. My fingers always seem to know where to go for the right notes and keys. My mind could never think through, in real time, where my fingers should go—this is obviously a spiritual event. I credit the Lord for this talent that he has given to me, beginning at the ripe-old age of seventy, and I believe in using my talents to the fullest as he so directs. Thank you, Lord, for building a talent in me at such an advance age. May I never stop praising you for it! I often joke that when I had my heart attack, the doctors discovered that:

There's within my heart a melody,
Jesus whispers sweet and low:
"Fear not I am with thee. peace be still"
In all of life's ebb and flow.

Jesus, Jesus, Jesus
Sweetest name I know.
Fills my every longing,
Keeps me singing as I go.

—Text and Music by Luther B. Bridgers

(I suggest you Google "He Keeps Me Singing" and listen to Bill and Gloria Gaither with Jake Hess.)

Soon after I found the Lord in my life I felt compelled to, in my spare time, establish a ministry for those needing work on a daily basis. Many of them were homeless and, with the economy being down, jobs were hard to find. I became friends with a family falling in this category, a couple with one adult son and his elementary son. The parents professed a belief in the Lord, and I sensed that they knew the homeless condition and the market for day workers. As a result, we joined as a team and established New Faith Ministries, a nonprofit effort to match willing workers with daily employment. I funded and supervised the venture and my partners managed the operation. On Wednesday night, I conducted a Bible study for those who were interested. Much prayer went into this venture, including my pastor. As time went by, there were only three or four attendees at Bible study, but I continued when I was in town. We came to realize that there were a few significant issues that we have to contend with. The greatest challenge was drug usage, and the few in the study group were combating this addition.

As time went by, three of them ask the Lord in their lives to deal with their addition. Another problem that we experienced was the competition with other daytime employers that were taking advantage of these unfortunates and were not compassionate in their dealings. I was able to afford three well-used vehicles, and would go out to wherever to provide transportation to bring workers to our office in the morning, assign them their daily work assignments, take them to their job, pick them up at the end of the day, bring them to the office, pay them their daily wage, take them to the bank to cash their check, and deliver them back to wherever they were living. In six months, this endeavor built up to a maximum of forty-four people one day.

Katie and I decided to take a one-week sailing vacation, and when we came back we found that all three of our vehicles had been sabotaged and were inoperative. At the same time, the State of Florida Unemployment Office notified us of an audit regarding our payments of Unemployment Compensation, which we were faithfully making. Their audit consists of assigning their rate to each hour of every person every day, depending on the category of type of work. During those six months, we had *never* had even one reported injury, and we had paid many thousand dollars into the State office. It turned out that this history of no claims had no bearing on their audit, and the evaluation resulted in a claim of fifty-three thousand dollars of which was levied on me personally. Needless to say, this wiped out our personal savings and IRA accounts. In addition, the three individuals that I had led to the Lord were drawn back to drugs. What is this, Lord? I was doing this for you, and never expected to earn any income for myself!

The following Sunday, a friend in Sunday school class, who was not aware that I had just shut down the ministry, handed me a book and said she thought that I might like to read it. The book was titled *Good Morning Holy Spirit!* by Benny Hinn. That nailed it! I had no awareness of the Holy Spirit having any part to play in this attempt to please our Lord with my efforts. I had not sought his direction in establishing this ministry, as I thought that it was obvious that he would bless my efforts. What major lessons I learned and have been convinced that this was worth the amount of money involved. Even at that, it has taken another twenty-five years of trying to please our Lord, before I have finally come to the fully realize the power and presence of the Holy Spirit.

Have Thine own way Lord, have Thine own way.
Thou art the potter, I am the clay.
Mold me and make me, after thy will.
While I am waiting, yielded and still.

Have thine own way Lord, have thine own way.
Search me and try me, Master today.
Whiter than snow Lord, wash me just now,
As in thy presence, humbly I bow.

Have thine own way Lord, have thine own way.
Hold over my being, absolute sway.
Filled with thy Spirit, till all can see,
Christ only always, living in me.

—Adelaide A. Pollard

(I suggest Google "Have Thine Own Way,
Lord by Jim Reeves," sung by Jim Reeves.)

Chapter 10

SELF-EMPLOYMENT

During my travels for my St. Lawrence employment, in my desire to have the Lord during these trips I would always have a juice-only fast the first day out, committing the trip to the Lord, and another fast the last day of the trip in thanks for being with me along the way. This routine brought many blessings along, and the Lord clearly showed himself many times. One of the many surprises that he had for me was that I had, for a few years, been experiencing some type of allergy that would come up periodically. My face, or some part of my extremity, would puff up for a few days before disappearing. It was beginning to happen nearly every week. The thought that came to me was that maybe it was a food allergy. I decided that during one of my trips out, I would do a juice-only fast for five days to see if that would help, and they did go away! I then started to introduce foods one at a time, and in that way I isolated the problem foods. After this discovery, I then went to a certified nutritionist to have my system completely analyzed for minerals, vitamins, and other nutritional elements. The results were extensive and revealing. From these results, the nutritionist prescribed the needed supplements to address these issues. I took them faithfully. After about three months the supplements ran out and I realized then that I was not having any allergic reactions of any kind! My allergies had been reactions to all types of cheese, ice cream (but not milk), nuts of all kinds including peanut butter, and orange juice (but not grapefruit juice). From that time for the next seven years, I could eat all of the previous restricted foods with the exception of walnuts. And then, the allergies came back. Testing resulted in a diagnosis that the culprit was my stomach, as it was not completely digesting the foods properly. After a few months of prescribed supplements, I was back to being able to eat everything again without any restrictions. In other words, my body returned to the way God designed me to be. I am especially pleased that the Lord healed my digestive track that, in turn, should help the rest of my body to be healthy. At my age at eighty-four, that is probably why I have no aches or pains of any kind and I sleep like a baby. Thank you, Lord, for helping me to be properly diagnosed, leading me to the right nutritionist, and then provide healing and great health.

One event happened during a return business trip through the Pensacola, FL, area in the early evening after dark. I was driving on I-10 and as I approached a bridge/overpass, I noticed sparks on the roadway ahead. As I came up to it, I discovered an extension ladder had apparently fallen from a vehicle, and I was unable to avoid it in time before hitting it. One rear tire blew out but I was able to safely make it to the side of the road. I put on the donut spare tire, but it was under-inflated and blew out before I made it to the next exit. Again, I pulled to the side of the road and parked. I noticed a house with a light on in the back, just across the fence. I climbed the fence, but as I walked toward the house I had a very strong feeling that I shouldn't be there, so I went out along the fence to the heavy-duty metal gate in the front of the house, climbed over it, and went to the house across the street. A man came to the door, and he offered to go back to the interstate highway to get my tire and take me to a tire dealer that was still open not far away. As we drove there, he asked me how I got to his house and I explained going first to the backyard of the house next door. He was visibly shaken as he explained that that family had two viscous pit bull dogs that were always in the backyard, but apparently the owner had them inside to feed them. Hallelujah! He stayed with me until I was able to get back on the road again to get home that same night. Lord, I know you were with me to provide protection from the accident and from the dogs, and for the Good Samaritan's assistance in resolving the issues needed to get me on the road again.

As time went by, I realized that my schedule of appointments, while on the road, had the Lord in it as well. One important appointment, in the Salt Lake City area, was located some distance away from where I stayed overnight. I had set the meeting time with plenty to spare, as I was traveling across the city, and much construction activity was going on in preparation for the Summer Olympics. I got a late start from the motel as a result of a long phone discussion with the company. As a reminder, this was is in the days before GPS, and navigation was by maps. Despite the late start, taking a wrong exit requiring me to go about ten miles out of the way, a detour off I-80 in the heart of the city, having two exits closed, the map not being up to date with added roads leading to the simulator center where the meeting was held, I still arrived with about ten minutes to spare. Remember, this is in the days without cell phones, and I would not have been able to call ahead if I was lost of delayed.

After a couple of years of being extensively on the road, I was home running an errand and stopped at an intersection, awaiting the green light. When the light changed I proceeded to cross this two-lane intersection and suddenly a car came at cruise speed between the cars on the right, hit my right front fender, and spun us both around. Neither one of us was injured, but my nice Mercury Cougar was damaged enough that it needed to be towed away by the insurance company to a parking lot. A few days later, we were notified that the car was totaled and, therefore, the state would not allow it to be repaired and re-licensed in Florida. Although the car was in beautiful condition otherwise, it was condemned primarily because it had such high mileage, over 170,000 miles. I was then advised to drive to the lot (about thirty miles away) to get our belongings out of the car. The next day we did so, and it just happened to be on Katie's birthday, a very tearful event as we really loved the car. When the accident happened I, strangely enough, did not have anger in my heart, and instead had a sense that everything would eventually be okay. When the meager amount of insurance came, I went down to the Credit Union that we had done business with for several years, to see how much of a loan that we could get for another car. We were informed that, because our employment had changed to commissions only, I would have to provide them with the IRS tax reports for the last two years of income. Since these reports did not show significant income to support any kind of loan, I was denied. This gave me a resolve to only purchase a car that we could afford to pay with cash from now on; a lesson that we needed to learn! With the insurance payment, we were able to purchase a well-used car that would meet our needs. This lesson has served us well through the years as we have always had good, decent-looking, reliable transportation while saving a considerable amount of money on loans and insurance payments. I am very grateful, Lord, for these lessons that continue to serve me well!

With the well-used car that I purchased, I was driving through Arizona on a trip west, in the middle of next-to-nowhere. Suddenly a serious tapping noise in the engine occurred while I was on an interstate. I was able to make it to the next exit, on the edge of a very small town. When I exited, a restaurant was right there and I went in and asked a waitress if there was a garage somewhere nearby. She directed me to a car dealership in town and suggested that I ask to see a certain mechanic that she named, and to mention her name. I was concerned that, based upon the seriousness of the noise, that it would take a few days to resolve. I did as she suggested, and the mechanic was able to fix the problem in a matter of a few hours and the cost was very reasonable. Thank you, Lord, for leading me to the right waitress, to the right garage, to the right mechanic, and for the costs being affordable.

On a business trip up the east coast, I departed on Monday morning, planning on client visits during the week, and be in Connecticut for the weekend at our daughter Jennifer's home. When I left Tampa, I was experiencing a shoulder ache that was with me day and night, and a friend suggested that I pop an Advil to relieve the pain. I did so starting Monday night to help me sleep, but the pain persisted, so I popped another one a few times through the night. This went on for three nights and on Thursday I began experiencing bleeding in my stool. I did not attribute it to the Advil but decided to terminate my customer visits and drive directly to Connecticut. I arrived late Friday and discussed with our daughter, Jennifer, my situation and desire to go to a walk-in clinic the next morning. The clinic advised me that they could not do anything, and that I needed to go to a hospital. At the hospital in New Britain, the doctor said that he could not treat the condition without going down with a probe into the stomach to determine the cause. I said that maybe I will just jump in the car and high-tail it to Florida for medical help near home. Jennifer happened to ask how long this procedure would take, and the doctor said that I would be out in three hours or less. So, I gave my okay to proceed. As he was conducting this procedure, the entire left side of my body went numb. This, of course, drew a crowd of medical personnel. For me I was completely at peace, as I clearly felt the presence of the Lord. In jest, I said to the doctor that I knew what was happening (the Lord being involved) and I would describe it to him when I got a chance at home. I also said to him, "Don't worry, Doc, I won't hold you to the three hours." The desire that was on my heart was to use this situation somehow as a witness, and I had nothing but joy and peace at the time.

As they wheeled me into the MRI machine, my prayer was, "Lord, I want to be a witness." Immediately, my numb left arm rose up off the gurney about eighteen inches and back down. What a surprise to me, but clearly the Lord did it as I did not think of such an act, and it was on the numb side of my body. Later the doctor said that he thought that I was just waiving to them. He said that he could not explain what caused my condition, that he had probably conducted twenty thousand of these procedures before without any such reaction, and that I would have to be admitted to the hospital for observation for the next few days. I ended up being there for four days, and I was completely at peace and reflected nothing but joy to everyone who came in. When I was discharged from the hospital, about 80 percent of my paralyses had disappeared, and I could easily drive back to Tampa. In a short time, I was back to normal without any prescriptions or therapy.

One of the first things that I did after being admitted to the hospital was to telephone my great friend, Ernie in Tampa, to ask for prayers. His wife informed me that Ernie was on his way to Cleveland to help with a situation that their son, Brian, had gotten himself into. Brian was living in Alabama while going to school. He was severely bipolar and had not been consistent in taking his medicine. Somehow, he had decided to fly to Cleveland, for an unknown reason, and while en route he had become unruly and had to be suppressed in-flight. Upon arrival at Cleveland, he was taken in custody, and Ernie was en route to do what he could do to help. Ernie knew of no one there as he had never been to the city. Lying in the hospital, I was somehow "inspired" to reach out to him. This was, of course, long before cell phones. I somehow called the hotel where Ernie had reservations but had not checked in yet. I then found out the hotel fax number. I have absolutely no recollection how I was able to rewrite, type, and fax to Ernie, a revised Psalm 139 that fit our circumstances. "Where can I go from your Spirit? If I go to a hospital in Connecticut, you will be there. If I go to Cleveland you will be there," etc. When he checked in, he was given the fax. As he was going up the elevator to his room, he was riding with what turned out to be an attorney who was able and willing to represent Brian, to be released from jail and return home in a few days. This was, again, a very clear answer to prayer! How impressive, Lord, to orchestrate such events and help us in our desperate time of needs!

During what turned out to be my final days of employment with St. Lawrence, an annual simulator symposium was held in Seattle, Washington. En route, I stopped to visit a friend in Ogden, Utah, and to visit Hill AFB. During this visit, my friend and his wife took me out to a very nice steak restaurant in the foothills nearby. During this dinner, a piece of meat stuck in the lower part of my esophagus. This did not affect my breathing, but prevented any food or drink from going into my stomach. I declined going to the hospital as I believed that it would pass in time. I struggled with it all night in a nearby motel, and all the following day as I progressed on with the trip. During the early evening, I arrived at a small town in Eastern Oregon, and there I checked into a motel. I still had the problem that, by now, was very uncomfortable and needed medical attention. This town, Ontario, only had a population of approximately 10,000 people. I inquired as to whether they had a hospital and was directed to St. Marks Catholic Hospital nearby. This was a very nice, new facility with friendly people, and I seemed to be the only one in the

ER. By now it was early evening. After discussing my condition and my need to keep expenses to a minimum, they called in a doctor who came in with his medical assistant. The blockage was confirmed by a probe, and the meat was extracted. To minimize the cost to me, they let me stay in the ER area for a few hours until the anesthesia wore off. I was okay by midnight and was dismissed. I was able, thereby, to stay overnight in the motel, that kept hospital costs to a minimum. What a huge blessing to find a hospital in such a small town and be able to get immediate medical attention at minimum expense.

During this time of employment, health insurance was a very real concern. When I started with St. Lawrence, the policy that I established with Blue Cross/Blue Shield was rather reasonable at about $250 per month for the two of us. Within a few years, the premium jumped to $480 and, when it jumped to $725 I knew it was no longer affordable. As a result of my prayer time, I somehow became aware of a Christian approach of sharing costs by Samaritan Ministries. This program is only offered to dedicated Christians, confirmed by my pastor, with no serious preexisting conditions. The cost per month was only $275. Payments are not made by Samaritan Ministries. Instead, their office divides the amount into enough members that they provide direct payments to the recipient who needs reimbursement, along with a note of encouragement and a promise of prayer. It was a wonderful, cost-effective program that has by now been expanded significantly without very much higher premiums than twenty years ago when we were in the program. We used it one time to pay for the costs at Ontario, described above, and all of our costs were defrayed by others. Whoever you inspired, Lord, to create such a program to minimize medical costs for committed Christians is another huge blessing!

The arrangement that I had with St. Lawrence for this symposium was to have a hospitality suite during the afternoon and evening of this event, and that I would split the cost 50-50 with the company. My technical counterpart at the company, Jim, came out with his model airplane (four-foot wingspan) as a conversation piece at the hospitality suite that I arranged. The symposium went off very well, and at the conclusion, while we were disassembling the suite, Jim then told me that he had been directed to notify me that my territory was now restricted to west of the Mississippi River, and that I was to send all of my customer contact information to the office. This was not a very subtle way to inform me that my services were no longer wanted. Here I was, at the other end of the country, with a bill to be paid for one-half of the costs for the hospitality suite. I was expected to send all of the customer information to the company that I had developed at my own expense during the six years of employment, at the same time having a relationship that St. Lawrence wanted to terminate. What had happened was that the father that had founded and built the business had passed away; his daughter took over the business and was taking all of the assets from the company and shutting it down. After prayerful consideration, I complied with all of their requests and ended my relationship with them in an amicable way. I knew, clearly, that the Lord was the one who got me this employment with St. Lawrence. He demonstrated that in a way that changed my life forever. He was with me at all times in a personal way during this employment, and he has helped me to grow hugely in my faith. I know knew and he has a better plan for me and will meet all of my needs.

I then prayed and acknowledged my faith in him in gratitude and dedicated myself toward whatever he had next in my life. I stated, emphatically, that I was going to wait him out. After about six weeks of waiting, he clearly answered my prayer, again, through my great friend, Ernie. As a realtor, he had a client that was selling her home and needed two rooms painted. Ernie knew that I was an experienced do-it-yourselfer and asked if I would like to do this work. I acknowledged that I would and, thus, began a new chapter in my life. In my prayers of appreciation to the Lord, I mentioned that I considered this employment as a ministry of helping people in need of home improvements, and that I expected him to do all of my marketing and scheduling. In that way, I would be willing to go where he wanted me to go, on his schedule, and to meet the needs of his people. I would do house painting and home repairs, and he kept me busy for the next nineteen years. This not only brought help to people in need, it provided employment for me in my own business, but also brought opportunities to bring many to a closer walk with the Lord. In addition, on occasion the Lord would bring individuals that needed employment to me, to work with me. Many of these events are discussed previously in Chapter 9.

This ministry continued until I was physically unable. When I turned eighty, Katie asked me how much longer that I expect to work like this. My response was that I hoped another ten years as it was keeping me in great physical condition, I was definitely helping others as a ministry, and it was helping me grow in my faith. Within two weeks, I came down the ladder after finishing painting a two-story home, and my knees told me that was the end of not only painting with ladder work but home repairs as my knees were too uncomfortable. Thus dramatically ended my ministry and began what turned out to be a year of transition, as described in Chapter 17.

> Cast all your cares, cast all your cares,
> Cast all your cares upon Jesus.
> He is truly able, so just leave them there,
> Cast all your cares upon Him.
>
> —Gary Oliver
> Based on Scripture 1 Peter 5:7

(Suggest Google "Cast All Your Cares"; uploaded by Danny Hood)

Chapter 11

HOUSE PAINTING AND HOME REPAIRS

After my employment with St. Lawrence ended, I was completely devoted to seeking the Lord for what plans he had for me. I was deeply in prayer for direction without any preconceived ideas. After about two weeks, my good spiritual friend, Ernie, called. His real estate business was succeeding, and he said that he had a woman who wanted two rooms painted. Ernie said that he knew that I was a good do-it-yourselfer and ask me if I would like to do this work. This led me to my next career, doing house painting and home repairs. I devoted this business totally to the Lord, with an understanding that I wanted him to do my marketing and scheduling so that I went where he wanted me and on his schedule, not mine. This led to a nineteen-year career of helping people and, at the same time, pro-viding for our needs. The Lord has designed me with a very large amount of empathy for others, thus the name for our sailboat. The most important thing, to me, was that I could be in people's lives and help them with their needs, while seeking how the Lord would use me to minister to them, if anything.

All of my prospects came through church friends, word of mouth, or from Ernie's clients. In order to ensure that the potential work was not by my doing, I intentionally never sought business on my own. Additionally, when I gave the client a written proposal for the work, I would never follow up to push the sale; if the Lord wanted me to be there, he would so motivate the client to enlist my help. This approach would, therefore, help ensure that he wanted me there, on his schedule, and for reasons that may by more than just to perform the work. The work that I performed was done "the old fashion way" with quality work and efforts that exceeded the client's expectations. I did so with an attitude that I was working for the Lord, so I did not want to do shoddy work. Also, he may have me there to do more that to just perform the work. I found that every day was different, and often I found a "calling" to befriend them, and encourage them through difficult times that they may be going through.

When living in Binghamton, our house was built on a hill, had a full basement, two stories, and a walk-in attic. It needed painting and I had purchased a forty-foot ladder for the job. On the down-hill side of the house, I had to place the bottom of the ladder in the next-door driveway that was at the level of our basement floor. The ladder, then, extended as far as it would go and at the top was a roof overhang that had to be painted along its edge. This was, essentially, four stories from bottom to top. I couldn't afford to pay someone to get up there, so I forced myself to suppress my fear, but I was shaking severely. When I came down, I disassembled the ladder and cut the top part in two as I was determined to never do that again! Amazingly enough, when I began my new career of house painting and home repairs, my fear of heights was gone—totally! The only way I can account for this phenomena is that when I asked the Lord into my life six years prior, he took away my fear, which is one of his promises. Scripture clearly states that there is no fear when the Lord is in control.

This work had the added benefits of keeping me physically fit and mentally challenged. I painted two-story houses, often with a peak that went to the end of my twenty-two-foot extension ladder. Occasionally, the peak would be over a pool screen. I engineered a way to support the pool frame, place an extension ladder on top of the frame, and then lay plywood on the ladder to provide a walkway. On top of the walkway, I would often have to place a stepladder in order to reach the peak. I would always be glad when the painting was finished, but I never had a "fear" of being up some twenty-five feet above the pool.

Soon after I started this business, I offered to organize a crew of church volunteers to paint the inside of the sanctuary and adjacent entranceway of our church. The sanctuary was large enough to seat approximately six hundred people, and the ceiling was about thirty feet high. The entranceway had a high ceiling as well. We used scaffolding for the main sanctuary, but for the entranceway we used a church-provided thirty-foot extension ladder. For my high-ladder work, I had purchased a ladder stabilizer that attaches to the top and extends to the side and toward the wall. This is very effective in stabilizing the ladder from side to side. My son, Bob, had just completed college and was temporarily working with me in my painting business. He was painting the entranceway along the ceiling, when suddenly the bottom of the ladder slid back, and Bob rode it to the floor. The stabilizer bent and absorbed much of the impact, but Bob sustained a serious cut just under one kneecap. He was rushed to the hospital and declared okay except for a one-inch deep cut about four inches long, and was stitched up and sent home. The amazing thing was this injury did not cut any muscle or tendon, and did not bruise any bones. Later, I had three individual people come to me and relate that they knew of people who experienced similar accidents and they all sustained broken backs. Thank you, thank you, Lord for saving Bob from serious injury!

Interesting enough, I had been singing in a men's quartet for a couple of years and at the end of each rehearsal, we would go to this entranceway and sing our four-part harmony to "Holy, Holy, Holy," that left us with goose-bumps, as the sound would reverberate so beautifully. I believe that we had clearly declared the entranceway holy ground, thus saving Bob from disaster.

I never sought to employ others, as I considered it my ministry alone as the Lord would develop it. One Sunday afternoon while I was working in my front yard, a lady, Deb, and one of her sons walked by and I introduced myself. They lived about four houses down the street, but I had never known them. She was, obviously, very troubled and I invited her to come back in a few hours for a talk in order to get to know her better. This event occurred in early September, and I found out that they had been living in their home all summer without any financial support, as her husband ran off in the spring, with his secretary, to live in Idaho. He took all of their funds including the children's college savings, and she had not been in the workforce for many years as she was a stay-at-home mom. They had lived without air-conditioning to save money, and food was scarce. She was so traumatized and depressed that she could hardly get out of bed. Although Deb was a college graduate with a bachelor's degree, she had been a stay-at-home mom for the kids that ranged from a freshman in Central Florida University to a ten-year-old boy. During the summer, the kids fended for themselves, and it was not clear to Deb where their food came from or how it got prepared, as she was in a fog.

I immediately brought her to work with me painting houses, and paid her an equivalent hourly wage to what I was charging for myself. This income provided enough for daily living expenses, but she would have to sell her house to meet her other expenses. Unfortunately, her house needed painting inside and out in order to get the most from the sale. As time and funds were available, I provided the materials for repairing and repainting the entire outside of the house. We then proceeded to repaint most of the inside, and the house was put on the market in early 2007. Soon, there was a cash offer her asking price, but before the sale was closed, a fire broke out in her bedroom from a shorted electrical in an outlet, about six o'clock in the morning. She happened to be up and taking a shower, and was able to escape without injury. As our Lord would orchestrate it, all of the children were visiting relatives and none were home. The fire destroyed the four bedrooms on the second floor, burned through the roof, and the smoke and water damaged much of the first floor. While the fire was being extinguished, Deb and I sat on the curb across the street crying and talking. I shared with her that I had a sense of peace and assurance that her troubles were about to bottom out, and better days were coming.

Katie and I then invited Deb and the boys to come and stay with us, and her daughter was already living at college. After about a month, the insurance provided for the rental of living accommodations for them, while repairs were accomplished. Deb went out for bids for the work to rebuild her home, and an "acquaintance" got the contract for a set amount of money. Discussions were held with him that I was willing to work with him on some of the effort, in order to make sure that all the necessary work was before exceeding the budget. As time went by, he did not use me, some extras were added by Deb, and he ran out of money before the job was completed. Therefore, before the occupational inspection could be done, I had to install all of the necessary baseboards and accomplish some of the final painting and touch-up. As we might remember, 2008 was the year of the now-famous housing crash, and the economy took a major nosedive. Amazing enough, soon after putting the house on the market, she had a buyer at her asking price. Thank you, Lord, that we were able to rebuild her home and that she got her asking price!

After working with me for nearly two years, she was offered a job with a veterinarian friend, with working conditions much more to her liking. After a few more years, she moved to Georgia to be near her family then got a teaching job with benefits, and now three of her children have completed college and have families. Here we are, ten years later, and all of this has been accomplished through the Lord's guidance and provision, and without one penny of child support or financial aid from her ex-husband or the government. Deb is a firmly committed Christian, and she actively proclaims her faith

Somehow, I was introduced to a Spanish-speaking church about tem miles away, to a men's Saturday morning breakfast. At the breakfast, the person in charge, Pete, and I got into a discussion about the experience that I had when I asked the Lord into my life. He was very interested and willing to pray and invited the Lord into his life. That was about fifteen years ago, and he continues to grow in his faith. He and his family joined our church and have continued to be faithful since.

A lady in our Sunday school class, Carol, invited me to give a quotation for painting the outside of their home. Her husband, Jerry, was not a church attender, and he had contracted a condition called

COPD. This illness affects all of his joints at all times day and night. Usually, I can accomplish whatever necessary repairs and painting in two weeks. I started this work the first week in December. When I checked in, Jerry invited me in for coffee. I usually decline as I am anxious to get on with the project, but this time I accepted. Carol was beginning her effort of baking cookies and goodies for the holidays. Of course, we were invited to indulge during the coffee break that turned out to be nearly an hour long. In the afternoon, we had another such coffee break and this became our daily routine. Jerry is the same age as me and also from Ohio. He had been in the Navy, had owned many boats through the years, and even a few sailboats. They were originally from Cleveland and sailed Lake Erie. He was also into computers and electronics, and I could always need help with such things. Because of his illness, the house needed some repairs before painting. Considering the daily coffee breaks, the holidays and weather conditions, and the repairs, the project took about six weeks. At the beginning of this project, it was obvious that Jerry was experiencing severe depression. After about two weeks, he became more positive, seemed more lighthearted, and seemed to have come out of his depression.

Jerry's spiritual commitment had been a serious concern to the family. During the Christmas Eve service a few weeks later, Jerry attended the service along with the family. To everyone's amazement, when the call was offered by the pastor to anyone who wanted to ask the Lord into their life, Jerry responded. It is now about seven or eight years later, I still go to his house nearly once a week for coffee and a chat when I am in town. His morale and humor continues to be excellent despite his significant health struggles. Hallelujah, thank you, Lord, that you have changed Jerry's life so significantly and, at the same time, have impressed on me the importance of a man-to-man friendship. Keeping such a friendship alive can have an effect on his enjoyment in life as well as his health and at the same time bringing meaning and joy in my life.

And then there was Mary. We became acquainted with Mary through our Sunday school class. She was burdened with a divorce, a grown boy who didn't want to grow up and leave home. She had few working skills, no alimony or child support, minimum income from working part-time, but was left with a small house that needed to be sold. It needed to be painted inside, and a new roof, but no money to pay for these improvements. I was led to help with these issues as well as to provide emotional encouragement. Deb was working with me at the time, and I had to pay for her efforts although I had to defray costs for this project until it was sold. I ordered the new roofing from Home Depot for Deb and me to install, but because the square footage was not large, the delivery company would not deliver the bundles to the roof, only to the driveway. The bundles were too heavy for Deb and me to carry them to the ladder and on to the roof. I, therefore, devised a slide up a ladder, with a pulley arrangement where we could get them up without over-stressing us.

When it came to painting the inside of Mary's home, to save money I took an empty five-gallon paint bucket and mixed leftover paint from other jobs that was off-white, and the resulting color turned out to be whatever. In this way, we had enough to paint the entire inside of the home without purchasing any more. The house sold in a short time, I got reimbursed for expenses, and we moved her into an apartment. Although this project still cost me my time, I consider it all coming from the Lord anyway, and we have always been well provided for. Scripture is clear that he will reward me in time.

I have a very good friend, Russ, who has developed his own ministry in Cuba and Haiti. Early on in this ministry, soon after I met him in Sunday school class, an individual near Tampa contacted Russ to let him know that he had purchased a ninety-foot freighter ship for the purpose of a ministry of helping the people of Cuba. It was anchored in the river near Palmetto, Florida, about one hour south of Tampa. It needed painting on the outside hull, and I volunteered to take on this project. It needed a special primer and final coat applied that was specifically formulated for salt water exposure. What an undertaking, as the work was done on a raft, with the bow being approximately twenty feet above the waterline. The work was done primarily by myself, but with some help from my son, Bob, and my brother Lyle. Upon completion, we were all on board when the ship was taken to the shipyard in Tampa, where donated goods were loaded in preparation of transporting to Havana. Unfortunately, the schedule for the trip was delayed due to complications from the U.S. State Department. When the trip was approved, I was not able to be on board, but it made history as the first freighter into the Havana harbor in forty-five years. The name of the ship is the *Carolina C*, as shown in the attached photo. Since that time, Russ has single-hand-edly established the largest ministry in Cuba and has also done great things for the Lord in Haiti.

My ministry/business continued for nineteen years until I was age eighty. On my birthday, Katie asked me how much longer I expected to continue this work. I replied that I was in hopes for another ten years as I really liked the work, I liked being in other people's lives to help them with their needs, and it was a great way to keep in excellent physical condition. Within two weeks, I finished painting the outside of a two-story house and found my knees were complaining heavily. That immediately stopped me from home repairs as well as house painting. Thus I found myself in an unexpected period of transition that has continued now for nearly four years, while searching for the Lord's purpose for my remaining days.

Where He leads me, I will follow,
Where He leads me, I will follow,
Where He leads me, I will follow,
I'll go with Him, with Him all the way.

—Hymn composed by E. W. Blandy

Chapter 12

MUSIC MINISTRY

As years went by, I continued to "putts around" with pianos even though we did not own one during our time in the Air Force. When it came to Christmas holidays, it was especially hard not having one at home, but I would usually find one that I could occasionally play. When we were stationed in Germany, we lived on the airbase at Ramstein for one year. In the fall of the year 1964, I went to a music store in Landstuhl and rented a piano—a baby grand—and, unfortunately, we lived on the second story of an apartment building. They delivered it and we enjoyed it for the holidays but, six months later we were reassigned back to the U.S. Those poor delivery guys from the store had to take it apart again and take it away. While at Ramstein, I participated in the Chapel Men's Group and was president of the group for one year. When approaching the Christmas holidays, I designed and we built a scene for the chapel lawn consisting of an organist, a choir director, and three singers. We mechanized the organist and choir director such that the organist hands moved back and forth over the mocked-up piano keyboard, and the choir director's arms moved up and down. A very unique fun project.

After I resigned from the Air Force, I accepted a job in Montoursville, Pennsylvania, as a company copilot for a small manufacturing company that was just purchasing a brand new Beechcraft twin-engine airplane. When the Christmas season came, we did not have a piano available but I was able to borrow an accordion from a friend, and learned it enough to be enjoyable for Christmas carols.

One year later, I landed a job in flight simulation that was less than one hundred miles away in Binghamton, NY.

Soon after we arrived in Binghamton, we purchased an older upright piano. My grandmother Griffin, who had paid for my piano lesson offered to buy an organ of my choice in order to encourage me further in music. I purchased a new Conn home model that I played nearly every day. The organ required a different technique and I then taught myself to play chords as it came with a book of fundamentals. At that time, the job that I had was very stressful and demanded many long hours of overtime. I never wanted to miss the dinner hour with the family, so I would typically either bring work home or return to the office after dinner. I would very often come home quite stressed out, go to the refrigerator for a beer, and then go to the organ to play and relax while I consumed my beer. When I had finished my beer, I was ready to face the family issues, and dinner. This was typically my routine, and many years later I was at a local Polish Polka concert where I found the kid next door was playing in the band and was excellent at the accordion. In talking with him later, he told me that he had been inspired as he grew up hearing me play the organ that was next to the window looking out to their house. Unbeknown to me, he had been taking lessons and had become a very accomplished musician. You never know who is watching you and what you do!

Throughout our married life, Katie and I always joined the choirs in the various churches that we attended. It was so very enjoyable to make music to our Lord, but it was also a great way to make friends and to encourage others. As I write this book, I am still active in our church choir at the age of eighty-four, and occasionally play the piano in different churches that I attend when I travel.

As my four kids were growing up, I strongly encouraged each of them to take at least two years of piano, after which they could decide whether to continue or not. Three out of the four kids endured their two years and then dropped the lessons. In later years, they all regretted that they stopped playing. The youngest, Bob, took up the saxophone in middle school, starting in seventh grade, and played all the way through high school. When he was in seventh grade, he rode the bus to a downtown school in the mandatory bussing days in Tampa. The sax was nearly as big as he was, so I mounted a set of wheels on one end of the case so that he could roll it without having to carry it. He didn't mind at all. This was well before luggage came with wheels.

I was a strong believer that music was to be appreciated and enjoyed. In eighth grade, Bob's music teacher required that they practice at home thirty minutes each day, seven days each week, and the parents were required to sign a form attesting to that fact each day. I ended requesting a teacher conference, insisting that this was unfair as it provoked a negative attitude toward music. No one should be required to do anything seven days a week. As a parent, we were not going to sign something that we were not going to require. She did not agree with my position and said that she was not going to change the requirement, but she soon changed it to six days.

We were so pleased that Bob took to music, as the high school class size was over six hundred students. Music gave him a small group that he could more easily make friends with, to find an identity with, and enjoy. He ended excelling in the marching band, the concert band, and the jazz band and made some lifetime friends in the meantime.

Music is clearly one of God's creations, and the Bible is full of references to sing and make music that pleases him. To play an instrument well not only requires physical skills but encourages and inspires a spiritual element that, at times, can seem miraculous. In all of the piano playing that I had done for over seventy years, I never felt really inspired. I enjoyed it for my own benefit, but I never felt comfortable playing for others. At age seventy, it all changed dramatically.

When I turned seventy, I happened to sit down at the piano and I somehow played a chord variation with my left hand that sounded good. After playing around with it, I found that I could play the melody with my right hand and fill in with chording with the left hand, and then, in time, some chords in the right. Soon I was playing a hymn by ear that was familiar, but with my own updated variation that sounded great. I was so encouraged by this discovery that I would every day play some of the old hymns that would come to mind. I stopped playing from printed music, and for the next eight years I continue to expand my repertoire of hymns. At that time, I decided that the Lord gave me this talent for a purpose, and Katie and I then started a sing-along at retirement care facilities. I would print out two verses of each of about fifteen hymns and make copies for everyone. She would be the one to organize everyone, getting them on the right page, and be the stand-up master of ceremonies (and comedian as she had a great sense of humor). We did this once a month for the last few years that she was still with me.

One day, I came to realize that in the morning as I was getting dressed, there would be a hymn or song that had been running around in my head until I finally addressed it. It was usually a hymn, but occasionally a popular song that had some meaning in my life. I could usually recognize the title but often would have to struggle to find it. It did not have anything that my brain had created and came to realize that it was a spiritual thing that could only come from the Holy Spirit. Recently, songs came to me on two separate days that I called my buddy Ernie to help identify them. One was "You Don't Need to Understand You Just Need to Hold His Hand." With Ernie, this was especially meaningful as this relates to the statement that I made to him when he was encouraging me to give my heart to the Lord. "I am an engineer, so if I can't understand it how can I expect to believe it?" Ernie's response was, "You are asking to know the mind of God. Give it up, just believe in him." I did and I've never been the same.

Recently when I was driving to church on Sunday, a song came to me in a powerful way:

> Let me call you sweetheart, I'm in love with you.
> Let me hear that you love me too.
> Keep your love-light burning in your heart so true,
> Let me call you sweetheart, I'm in love with you.

This provoked a discussion with the Lord while I was driving, "What does this mean? You know that I have no one in my life since you took Katie that I can sing this to."

He replied, "This song is for you!"

After Katie was taken to her home in heaven, I still continued for a few months with my own ministry, but it just wasn't the same. During this time my brother, Lyle, encouraged me to continue with my music ministry as he stated that we never know who will be touched by this music. I especially enjoyed playing in the memory care unit of two of the retirement facilities. I found such a loving desire from the residents for me to play, and they were very enthusiastic. The first time that I played in one of the homes, a little lady came to me while I was playing and hugged me and hung on to me while I continued playing. After I concluded the hymn that I was playing, a care giver came over with a chair and had her set right next to the piano. Each session that I played I came away with more joy than when I came.

Another facility that I have enjoyed playing at was an adult daycare facility in Tampa called Pyramid. This facility is for adults only, initiated by the State of Florida but also supported by several churches in the area. Daily (five days each week), these "challenged" individuals would be brought by vans, cars, busses, and however they could get there for daily activities of all sorts—arts, crafts, singing, technical, drama, and the like. This facility even accepts individuals that cannot take care of their own personal needs and has staff to assist. In addition to the activities, lunch is provided. A church service is conducted once each week for whoever wants to participate, as well as a Canine Ministry with Service Dogs. I would come once each week to play a beautiful grand piano in the entranceway that is the confluence of the hallways. I would try to be there as they are finishing lunch, and then they could bring a chair and sit around the piano. I would give them about a thirty-minute concert of various types of music. This they greatly enjoyed, especially seasonal music, and the music can be heard throughout the facility. Get this—this facility supports an average of about 160 of these challenged adults each day, with a very loving and caring staff and a very nice, adequate facility.

In more recent years, I have expanded my repertoire to include popular songs of the '40s and '50s that I grew up with, and that Katie and I had as love songs. I discovered a love song that we especially enjoyed, and it was written such that it could be interpreted either secular or religious. It is "Have I Told You Lately That I Love You":

> Have I told you lately that I love you,
> Have I told you there's no one above you,
> You fill my heart with gladness,
> Take away all my sadness,
> You ease my troubles, that's what you do.

> —Rod Stewart

I very often play and sing this song, two verses. The first is to the Lord and the second is to my dear Katie.

I have come to realize that Louie Armstrong, the noted jazz performer, made famous two songs that we all (my age group) are familiar with, but most do not recognize as spiritual—and we should:

> When the Saints Go Marching In

> O, when the Saints go marching in,
> I want to be in that number
> When the Saints go marching in.

> What a Wonderful World

> I see trees of green, red roses too
> I see them bloom for me and you
> And I think to myself, what a wonderful world

> I see skies of blue and clouds of white
> The bright blessed day, the dark sacred night
> And I think to myself, what a wonderful world

> The colors of the rainbow so pretty in the sky
> Are also on the faces of people going by

I see friends shaking hands saying how do you do
They're really saying, "I love you."

I hear babies crying, I watch them grow
They'll learn much more that I'll never know
And I think to myself, what a wonderful world
Yes I think to myself, what a wonderful world.

For a treat, Google these songs and listen to Louie Armstrong sing them.

I feel so inspired when I am able to see through people into their loving hearts, as I play and sing hymns and popular songs. My belief is that every one of the composers of these songs and hymns were inspired by our Lord when they were composed. I feel so privileged to be able to play such music, to help convey God's inspired love for us all. Oftentimes, whenever I travel and go to a church, if there is no music being played ten minutes before starting the service, I will go to the piano and play whatever the Lord brings to mind. If the music director or pastor is there, I will ask for permission, but if not I will just begin playing anyway, and I have never been given anything but appreciation. Recently, one of my friends at my hometown church expressed that he could listen to my playing all day long. How very encouraging, and I usually get applause—not that I take it for pride, but I am encouraged and amazed that beginning at age seventy, the Lord could develop such a talent with me for lifting the spirits of others. When I can, I joyfully explain that this playing is clearly a miracle, as I do not memorize any song and, obviously, I cannot think where each finger should go as I play. I amaze myself continually with my playing, and the unique opportunities that I have to bring glory to him.

I have always played at home on an upright or spinet piano and have cherished the opportunity of playing on a baby grand or grand piano. Two years ago, as of this writing, on a Thursday a picture came up on Facebook from a great friend, Nancy. The picture was of a unique and beautiful bookshelf made from the shell of a baby grand piano that her parents had hanging on a wall in their home. I texted her back on Friday, jokingly asking where the guts of the piano were—I would love to play it. The next day, Saturday, in an unrelated Facebook posting, another friend posted a picture of her baby grand piano that she was offering for sale. It had not been played for years, and it was just taking up space. I called her and found that the price was very reasonable, and I offered to come the next day and purchase it after I played it. I felt that the Lord was inspiring me with this instrument, as an encouragement to continue with my talents. The piano was in beautiful condition, and after researching the history, found that it was 113 years old. It was built by the owner of a company devoted to building the highest quality piano possible, using the best of materials and workmanship. He built an entire town around a plant. Homes were constructed for the employees and offered for sale to them for the cost of materials only, and on a payment plan.

Thank you, Lord, for my talent and my inspiration to proclaim your grace in my life to all who want to hear.

> How can I keep from singing Your praise
> How can I ever say enough, How amazing is Your
> love.
> How can I keep from shouting Your name,
> I know I am loved by the King
> And it makes my heart want to sing.
>
> I will lift my eyes, in the darkest night.
> For I know my Savior lives.
> And I will walk with You, Knowing You'll see me
> through,
> And sing the songs You give.
>
> I can sing in the troubled times, Sing when I win.
> I can sing when I lose my step and fall down again.
> I can sing 'cause You pick me up, sing 'cause
> You're there,
> I can sing 'cause You hear me, Lord,

When I call to You in Prayer.

I can sing with my last breath, Sing for I know,
That I'll sing with the angels, and the saints
around the throne.

—Text by Eithne Ni Bhraonain
Music by Nicky Ryan and
Roma Shane Ryan

(Google "How Can I Keep from Singing"
and sing along with Chris Tomlin.)

...be filled with the Spirit, speaking to one
another with psalms, hymns, and songs from the
Spirit. Sing and make music from your heart to
the Lord, always giving thanks to God the Father
for everything, in the name of our Lord Jesus
Christ. (Eph. 5:18)

Chapter 13

FLORIDA TO ALBANY, NY

Cast Off

*Twenty years from now you will be more
disappointed by the things that you didn't do than
the ones you did do. So, throw off the bowlines.
Sail away from the safe harbor. Catch the trade
winds in your sails. Explore! Dream! Discover!*
— *Mark Twain*

Now that we had gained more experience and confidence in long-distance sailing, we decided to take on a two-year voyage from Florida to the Upper Peninsula, Michigan, near where Jim lives and sails. The first summer was a three-month trip from the Jacksonville, Florida, area to Albany, NY, where we would store the boat, and the next summer from there to the Upper Peninsula of Michigan.

The way began this great adventure was without fear and with great anticipation. Ever since my Air Force flying days, I have sought adventures dealing with new experiences and challenges. As I reflect back, I have never been impacted by fear even after surviving the near-misses of my life. What is it that separates me from others that experience fear that seriously impacts their lives? I am convinced in my mind, beyond a shadow of doubt, it is that as a teenager I asked the Lord Jesus to come into my life. As the Bible promises in many places, by doing so he will guide and protect you, he takes away fear and replaces it with joy.

He helped me as a teenager while taking flying lessons, when I experienced engine failure and landing in a field in Ohio. He helped me take on the huge challenge of going to the Military Academy at West Point even though I knew that I was ill prepared, academically, and while there I struggled each day to avoid failing. I joined the Air Force in the early days of single-engine jets, and as a pilot and flight instructor in eight years had my share of near disasters. I never experienced a fear of flying, through the extreme amount of bad weather in Europe, flying in formation even at night, through sand storms in West Texas, landing at numerous different airports throughout the U.S. and Europe—all with a very unsophisticated airplane that only had approximately 1.5 hours of fuel, with a bare minimum of lighting in the cockpit, and no amenities such as autopilot. I had no fear of the unknown as we sailed four all-night trips to the Bahamas, or as we sailed up the Intracoastal Waterway from Florida to the Upper Peninsula of Michigan. During the total of five months on this trip, we experienced groundings, some severe storms, serious challenges from tides, and probably a million rocks to navigate through.

Preparation

The first challenge in this adventure was preparing the thirty-year old boat. I updated it with a new paint job, installed a generator for power, and improved comfort, safety, and efficiency for storing everything that was needed for such a long trek. Money was an issue and, therefore, I did everything myself. Therefore, my only expense was the cost of materials.

A complete paint job was accomplished outside, and this required building a temporary plastic enclosure, taking the toe rails off, sanding the hull and deck. The entire surface was spray painted and immediately followed by rolling with a foam roller. Storage doors were installed in the cockpit for access to the lower bunk areas that were modified to become storage areas. A roller-reefing system was installed to ease the effort for operating the jib sail. This system eliminated the need to go to the bow when sailing, to raise and lower the jib sail. I loved this feature so much and would often mention so during the voyage. Katie remarked, after hearing it so many times, that she was concerned that I was going to divorce her and marry the roller-reefing system. A bimini frame was constructed with a canvas cover over the cockpit for shading us from the sun and providing some shelter from rain.

The inside areas were modified to accommodate plenty of galley food storage, an apartment-size refrigerator, a toaster oven, a new alcohol stove, and a portable generator. Two deep-cycle batteries were installed beneath the V-berth bunk that would power for the refrigerator.

Many of these tasks were daunting, especially never having accomplished them before. But I was inspired to do them, always convinced that whatever I got myself into, the Lord would help me accomplish them. As an example, I was challenged when it came to cutting into the fiberglass in the cockpit to install storage doors, installing the refrigerator, hooking up the generator and deep-cycle batteries, and installing storage drawers for food storage in the galley. Painting the hull and deck was a concern, to make it look like new and professional. I have learned that being inspired is a spiritual thing— being encouraged by the Holy Spirit. One of my favorite words, in addition to the boat name, *Empathy*, has been the word *enthusiasm*. In *Webster's Dictionary*, before it was modified to be "politically correct," one of the definitions was "…empowered by the Holy Spirit." Thank you with all my being for embedding this in my life, as this word, along with enthusiasm, has always defined my nature.

Navigation

Many charts and books were procured describing not only the route to follow but all of the marinas and facilities along the way. We also had descriptive materials telling us of the interesting towns and history of the areas that we were transiting. From this information, I planned the entire trip for each day, with room allowed for the Lord's intervention and the desire to explore and area longer. During the trip, up to 1.5 hour each evening was spent planning for the next day, including programming the GPS. This early-model GPS required manually entering each waypoint—latitude and longitude. A list of waypoints was not available at that time, so each one had to be measured off the charts. This was a daunting challenge as each chart had its own scale, and estimating the latitude/longitude accurately was quiet a chore. This device was a lifesaver, even though it was time-consuming and subject to my inaccuracies and mistakes. It continued to be a significant challenge throughout the trip.

The Adventure Begins!

We planned on tailoring the boat to Palatka, Florida, and launching *Empathy* on the St. Johns River that leads to Jacksonville, Florida. Bob, Michele, and Lauren (1 ½ years old) who live just east of Tampa, accompanied us in order to bring the trailer and van back after the boat was launched. We left Tampa Saturday morning for the four-hour trip. As we approached Palatka, about a mile out of town, Bob noticed that one of the trailer wheels was tilting. Upon inspection, we discovered that the wheel stub had become compromised with rust and was about to break loose. We carefully proceeded to the edge of the town of Palatka, where the wheel became too dangerous to proceed—not even the remaining one mile to the launching ramp. At this point, a motel was there with a parking lot available where we could park and work on the trailer. After checking out repair shops, we found one that could make two new axles if we could take the old ones off and being them in to be refurbished. This we were able to do and three days later we were underway again to the launching ramp.

After launching, Bob and his family departed for home as he had to be back for work. After they left, we had three obstacles to overcome before we could depart. The refrigerator was not cooling, the bimini (awning) had to be put up for shade, and the mast had to be raised. An "angel" appeared in a truck and helped find the right man to repair the refrigerator. We then had to wait for a week for the winds to die down so as to raise the mast. In the log of our experiences that Katie recorded each day of this adventure, "The two words that come to mind are perseverance and patience, and Dean portrayed these traits during this entire trip. I might confess that, as his first mate, I also grew through situations that tested my faith and endurance, and I became a better sailor for it." Thank you, Lord, for helping solve these challenges for us and giving us the courage to explore onward!

Starting the Voyage

The entire trip, from beginning to end, was in complete recognition that the Lord was our Captain, and we were constantly seeking his guidance and protection. For the two of us who were seventy-six years old at the time, the thought of the voyage could have been daunting. However, Katie had much confidence in me, and we both exhibited total trust in our Lord. The exciting thing about being outside of our comfort zone is when we clearly experience his presence. During the first three months of this adventure with its obvious exposure to the weather, we naturally experienced a few storms. Every time that we were confronted with heavy weather, we were either in a marina or a safe anchorage.

Captain Dean and Matey Katie

In order to depart Florida before the summer heat and humidity set in, we decided to depart April 10th of 2010. Katie and I were both seventy-six years old then, and we were as excited as teenagers. Katie's health had been without any illness, and I was full of energy and pronounced totally fit despite a heart attack that was corrected with a stint in 2007, and prostate cancer that was eliminated in 2008. Both incidences resulted in a clean bill of health and declared to be fully fit to continue normal activities.

Katie and I began the first morning, before departing the marina in Palatka, Florida, with prayer, scripture from the Upper Room, and personal prayers asking God for safety during the coming adventure. We trusted that he would be with us in all situations. We then, every morning thereafter, had as a routine to do likewise, to listen to the latest weather to guide us with our decision as to whether to venture out, or consider other alternatives. We later added daily exercises as was possible in the confines of the boat.

> God is our refuge and strength, an ever-present help in time of trouble. Therefore we will not fear, though the earth give way and the mountains fall into the heart of the sea, though its waters roar and foam and the mountains quake with their surging. (Ps. 46:1)

This adventure was an awesome opportunity to experience God's wonderful creation from the perspective of the waterway; the tides, the currents, especially in the outlets to the Atlantic Ocean, the intensity of storms, the beauty along the way, and his presence during times of trouble.

The St. Johns River was the first of hundreds of rivers and streams that we would encounter, some being two to three miles wide, others small ones winding through grasslands, and a few as large as bays that were so large that we could not see across. Each day, we traced our charts diligently, watching the depth sounder and GPS, and hoping for enough wind to be able to sail. Unfortunately, most of the time the winds were just off the bow or not enough to make headway, so we ended up motoring most of the 1,435 miles we traveled. Jacksonville, FL, was the first introduction to bridges of all types. Four major ones come to mind; bascule, lift, railroad and fixed. The chart always (except one) gave the height of an approaching bridge, and we knew that we needed thirty-two feet from the water's surface at low tide, to pass under them.

Our first hair-raising experience happened at Mayport, FL, just ease of Jacksonville, under very strong winds. We noted a marina on the chart where we could find protection from the winds. In the confusion of the situation, we entered a small inlet that we thought was the marina and discovered that it was not the right inlet. With the strong winds that we were encountering, we were barely able to turn around and exit. We then found the correct marina just east by about a mile. The significant tides and currents were the first time that we had encountered the likes of them, along with strong winds and waves. Katie was in the bow and later described it as a wild bronco ride. As we entered the shelter of the marina, we encountered a ferry boat that was jocking to enter his slip and we had to loiter until we could proceed into ours. Solid ground sure felt good. Thank you, Lord, for helping us be safe through this encounter.

The next day, as we proceeded north toward Georgia, we encountered white pelicans, gulls, and friendly dolphins to delight our journey through the grasslands. And at that very moment we saw the space shuttle overhead that was gliding in for a landing at the Kennedy Space Center. Thank you, Lord, for the perfect timing for us to see it travel overhead, coming from outer space!

A few miles before we got to Savanna, Georgia, we anchored for the night in a stream just off the Waterway. As we woke up in the morning, we sensed that the boat was not moving about, we realized that the stern was aground and that the tide was going out. I tried to motor off without success. By then, the bow was lowering nose down, but we were safe for however long it would take before the Lord would bring the water back up. We decided to enjoy the day anyway, and at low tide the boat was heading down at about a thirty-degree angle—what a strange experience but safe as the boat stayed erect. At about four o'clock in the afternoon, the tide had come up enough to float away. We found out later that there was a "moon tide" that night, when there was a full moon that causes the high and low tides to be excessive, and that probably contributed to our dilemma. Thank you, Lord, for such an unusual way of demonstrating your awesome power and faithfulness, while keeping us safe!

Another day, at Beaufort, SC, we tied up at the city marina for a walking tour of the town. A sign at the dock told us that we could not stay there overnight. In the late afternoon, we returned to the boat. When we backed away from the dock, I suddenly realized that the current was very strong and was forcing us back into the next dock that was filled with boats. One of the negative aspects of the boat design is that when the motor is placed in reverse and when power is applied, the flow of the water is applied against the back side of the rudder. In the excitement of the moment, I suddenly applied high power; the rudder twisted sideways and along with it snatched the tiller handle out of my hand. The handle jerked to the side against the metal hand railing and broke it off completely with only a stub remaining. I was able to control the motor at full power while I back away very slowly against the current until I had just enough room from the other boats to put the motor in forward gear and turn it sideways in order to turn the boat. I was just barely able to avoid the other boats and get underway out of the marina. I then found a mooring buoy that we could tie up to for the night. The next day, I found that I could modify the tiller handle enough that I could reattach it and, although it was a bit shorter, it was still functional. Thank you, Lord, for saving us from such a potential disaster and allow us to continue with the trip.

In North Carolina, we stayed at a marina at the very south edge of the Albameyer River and planned to get an early start in order to cross the wide bay where the river flows into the Atlantic. It was about thirty-five miles across the bay, which was a long day for us. We then needed to enter a very small river that was part of the Intracoastal Waterway. The weather was forecast to be light rain and up to 15 mph winds, which was moderately/high for us. These winds were favorable to travel (under motor), and we expected this crossing would take about eight hours. We are usually fair-weather sailors and this turned out to be a bit intimidating, with light rain, strong winds, and significant waves. As we approached the inlet to the small river, it was very difficult to pick it out as it blended in to the surrounding landscape. The accuracy of my old GPS, with my manually-calculated waypoints, was not that accurate, so I had a lot of anxiety. Suddenly, out of the light rain came a tugboat heading directly into the inlet of the river and disappeared behind the landscape. Perfect timing for leading us into the river. Thank you again, Lord, for providing such help in our time of need.

Another time as we came into Beaufort, North Carolina, there was a vacant floating mooring buoy that we tied up to for the night. This was amongst and alongside other buoys. After an hour or so, as we were about to go ashore, a man motored up in his small dingy, and informed us that someone had placed the buoy there, but it was only attached to a single cement cinderblock. This could have caused us a significant problem in the night when the tide changed and associated currents would have drifted us to who knows where. So, we moved to another buoy. Thank you again, Lord, for keeping us safe.

After we passed Norfolk and experienced the overwhelming size of the Navy ships in the shipyard compared to *Empathy*, the thought came that God created water that can float not only our eight-thousand-pound boat but also such a ship that may weigh eight hundred thousand tons or more. Amazing thing to contemplate!

After entering the Chesapeake Bay, it was nearing dusk as we searched for our anchorage for the night, on the west side of the bay. This bay is so large that you cannot see across it. The anchorage that I had planned was just before the Potomac River. Due to the winds, we selected the north side of the bay, for protection from the winds. After we anchored, it started raining and the winds changed direction whereby we were exposed to the winds. We, therefore, decided to motor to the southern shore hoping for better protection. By now it was dark and raining. Katie went forward to the bow and shinned our bright light into the darkness and rain. She suddenly yelled to stop, which I did, and we then realized that we were heading directly into a strange type of fence that projected out in the water quite a way from shore. We then turned away from the fence toward shore and dropped anchor for the night. The next morning, we discovered that this was some type of long net was stretched out some way from shore and held secure with metal posts. Apparently, this was a way to catch fish as they drifted through the net. This contraption was not lighted and we could have wound up with it around the boat and tangled in the motor. Many thanks to you again, Lord, that Katie was able to pick out this obstacle and that we were able to avoid this potential disaster while in the midst of the storm.

One time while in the Chesapeake, we learned that a storm was coming, so we headed to a protected area and anchored on the inside of Kent Island on the east side of the bay. Before the evening set in, I received a strong urge to find another anchorage and found on the chart a more protected area nearby to stay the night. We immediately moved before dark. The storm hit about eleven o'clock in the evening, and it was so strong that, at anchor, the boat would heal over on its side about twenty degrees of angle. This, of course, was very disconcerting, but I could use my GPS to show whether we were dragging anchor or not. Fortunately, we were secure. The next morning, we looked out to discover that the wind had flipped the dinghy upside down with the dinghy motor attached. I righted the dinghy and brought the motor on board. The water was, of course, salt water and the motor had been in the water overnight. I immediately cleaned everything that I could, drained the gas tank, added fresh gas, and it started up without delay. Thank you, Lord, for saving our motor and for our anchors holding us secure! In the morning, an older gentleman and his dog came out from shore in his fishing boat to check on us, and he said that his wind indicator showed that the winds had gusted to over forty knots. Thank you also, Lord, for sending someone who cared enough to check on us!

We picked up our grandson, Spencer, in Annapolis, MD, and headed out around the north side of Kent Island, and found a delightful bay to swim in and to stay overnight. Recent research has discovered that in the 1700s, there was a group of Quaker families from Switzerland that first landed on Kent Island, and may have stayed is this very bay. The Quakers were a religious Christian sect that were escaping persecution in Europe. In this group were some

Griffin families that, I believe, were early ancestors on my mother's side. If so, this would confirm that both sides of my family of ancestors came from Europe to find a country where they could live and worship freely, namely the Pilgrims on my father's side and Quakers on my mother's side. Wow! No wonder, Lord, that you are so prominent in my life, and you are now inspiring me to tell about your influence in my life, in this book!

Try as hard as we could to avoid going aground, we still managed to go four times. The waterway had not been maintained for over fifteen years, and sand had managed to fill it even in the marked channel. Three times we were able to rock the boat under full throttle in reverse and work our way free. One of them, however, the boat did not budge. The wind was rather strong, so I got the thought of putting up the main sail to see if it would heel the boat over enough to sail off the grounding, and it worked! Thank you, Lord, for bringing this solution to my mind without having to pay someone to pull us off.

In New Jersey, the waterway has not been extended to New York harbor. This meant that we had to go out in the open Atlantic for about twenty miles. Before we had to exit the waterway into the Atlantic, the bridges became too low for our boat to traverse with the mast up. I was not anticipating this to happen, however, for a few more miles. As we were motoring up, we approached a bridge that looked high enough for our mast, but it is always difficult to judge. Katie went down to read the chart as I was at the helm approaching the bridge. Suddenly, I had a very strong urge to reverse course. Just as I started to turn, I noted on the sign on the approach that the height was too low, and at the very same time Katie yelled to turn around. This all happened about five seconds before the mast would have crashed down with subsequent major damage. Thank you again, Lord, for your Holy Spirit helping us to avoid this potential disaster in the in the very last few seconds!

As we approached Staten Island, we discovered a beautiful bay on the south edge of Staten Island. It was very protected, large, and had numerous spare mooring buoys to tie up to. Above the trees on the east side, we could see the lights of the Verrazano Narrows Bridge at night, going from New Jersey to Brooklyn and on to New York City.

What a sight, and to think that we were actually that close to the Big Apple, safe in an anchorage that was free, as there was no indication as to where to pay a fee, and no one around to collect. We stayed for two nights.

The greatest thrill of this entire adventure was, after going under the Verrazano Narrows Bridge, to sail past the Statute of Liberty. This was definitely a spiritual experience as we were touched by actually being where millions of immigrants had sailed, coming for the first time to America—the only country ever dedicated to God, where we could freely live, to grow in his grace, and to be free to worship him as we were so inspired. Until recent years, with the advent of airline travel, everyone who came to our land of liberty and freedom traveled by boat. Just beyond the Statue of Liberty was Ellis Island, where our early pioneers all processed through. Thank you, Lord, for these great United States, and the freedom to sail in these waters in our little twenty-eight-foot boat, *Empathy*. Lord, may we never take for granted what you have blessed us with so abundantly!

I had made reservations at a marina in Jersey City, New Jersey, that was just beyond and within sight of Ellis Island. This marina was directly across the Hudson River from the Twin Trade Towers that had been destroyed by terrorism about nine years prior. We stayed two nights and were thrilled and felt extremely blessed to be there. While we were there, we shared lunch with Stan's high school friend Jim, whom I have previously discussed, his wife, and a son that lived nearby.

From here we proceeded up the Hudson River. As we were passing about half was up to West Point, I related to Katie that when I was a cadet over sixty years before, there were probably a dozen WWII Navy ships that were surplus and identified to be salvaged. In the meantime, they were anchored somewhere in this area. We decided to anchor and take a walk along the western shore in order to get some exercise. As we came ashore with our dingy and walked up to the small trail to begin our trek, we happened across a memorial plaque commemorating this event! Imagine, of all the miles of shoreline that we could have come to, we got led to this very spot. This was clearly a "God thing" for which I thank him immensely!

Our destination for this summer was Albany, New York, where we were to store the boat until the following year. Albany is about 150 miles from NYC, and we were informed when we arrived that we had less than one hour to prepare the boat to be taken out of the water for storage, due to the tides. We were at high tide, and they only had a window of two hours before the water would drop too low, and we would have to wait until the next day at high tide. We were barely able to get the mast down and prepare the boat to be taken out. As I contemplated later, I am amazed that God's tides could be so strong that the level of the river could be so affected 150 miles away. What an awesome power, that the gravity of the moon could lower the level of the waters in New York Harbor such as to affect the river over 150 miles away. And, that the precise order of your creation is so perfect that such tides can be predicted hundreds of years in advance. What an awesome God!

Fear Tomorrow(?)

I do not fear tomorrow!
For I have lived today;
And though my course was stormy,
My Pilot knew the way.

I do not fear tomorrow!
If the sails set east or west;
Or sea or safe in harbor,
In Him, secure, I rest.

—Phyllis Michael

Chapter 14

ALBANY TO UPPER MICHIGAN

Life's Sailing Goal

One ship sails east, another west,
With the self-same winds that blow;
Tis the set of the sails
And not the gales
Which decides the way to go.

Like the winds of the sea,
Are the ways of fate
As we voyage along through life;
Tis the will of the soul
That decides it's goal,
And not the calm or the strife.

—Ella Wheeler Wilcox

The second part of our great adventure began in early June of 2011, in Albany. Apparently, the winter had been a rough one as the plastic covering over the boat was completely shredded, but no damage was experienced. The Erie Canal began about fifteen miles north, further up the Hudson River. This waterway was completed in 1825 and is about 360 miles long. This was one of man's greatest accomplishments due to the distance it traversed, rugged terrain through New York and Pennsylvania, and the depth and width that was required for transporting barges both ways at the same time. The canal was completed in seven years, and had to be dug by hand, as this was accomplished long before the development of power equipment. A total of thirty-six locks were built in order to raise and lower the barges a total of 565 feet. As we traversed this waterway, we were struck with sense of history, in that our very own early pioneer families travel this very way. This canal allowed travel by water from Europe to Detroit and Toledo, avoiding overland travel by wagon over difficult terrain. This waterway also avoided Niagara Falls. The canal's peak year was 1855, when thirty-three thousand shipments were experienced. The reality set in that motors had not yet been developed; therefore, traveling through the canal required horses and mules to pull the barges, and all of the locks were operated by hand. Awesome to comprehend, and the concept that it could be done had to be inspired by God through those who were the decision makers of the day.

From the main waterway, a branch canal was added from outside of Syracuse, NY, to Oswego that allowed a way up to Lake Ontario. The second year that we had *Empathy*, 1980, we traveled this canal when we sailed from Ithaca, NY, on Lake Cayuga to the Thousand Islands on the St. Lawrence River. My mom and dad Bates were with us along this waterway and, although Dad had a serious case of Parkinson's disease was so pleased to have the experience of motoring *Empathy* in and out of the locks. What a great memory!

A few miles before Oswego, we tied up for the night at a small-town marina at Fulton, NY. This stop was on a Saturday afternoon, and found that we could walk to church for Sunday service. In church the next day, we met a very nice couple who was very interested in our boat. They invited us to meet up with them that afternoon in Oswego, as they would like to take us out to dinner. He was a retired professor at the university and wanted to show us around. After church, we launched off and made the short trek to Oswego. As we entered the marina, a coast guard boat pulled in behind us and requested permission to come aboard for an inspection. Who was I to deny such a request? The routine inspection revealed three minor issues that would require a trip to a marine store, and there was one a few miles away. The problem was having transportation. In a few minutes after securing *Empathy* in a slip, our new friends arrived, and they agreed to take us to the store. After that, they took us on a tour of the university and then dinner. Thank you, Lord, for finding such helpful friends along the way.

As we prepared to leave the marina the next day, a nearby power boater came over and asked if we were about to travel across the eastern end of Lake Ontario. He mentioned that he had never crossed such a big body of water and wondered if we could travel together. His name was Charlie, and he had a thirty-four-foot trawler, an older wooden boat named *Old Faithful*. He was with a friend, Joyce, and they were "Loppers"; that is that they were on a loop from Florida up the east coast, through the Great Lakes down through Chicago, and along rivers to the Gulf of Mexico, and then back to home at Ft. Meyers, Florida. Would you believe that, as I was ready to write this part of our adventure, I received a telephone call from Joyce who just got out of the hospital from having a pacemaker inserted? I have not talked to her in nearly two years. Lord, your timing for this communication is incredible!

The next day, Monday, we departed Oswego for Sackets Harbor, about an eight-hour voyage. The winds were perfect for sailing, and the seas were okay for our new friends. All went very well until we were nearing the marina. At that time, we had gone under motor, and suddenly the motor dropped down to idle. We shut it down for a few minutes and started it up again, and it ran normal into the marina. The next day, we proceeded to Alexandra Bay in the St. Lawrence River, where service should be available. En route, the motor shut down two more times, but we were very much assured by having our friends accompanying us. At Alexandra Bay, the motor was taken off and serviced, although they could not find anything wrong. Together, we proceeded along for the next month, and the intermittent problem continued, but having *Old Faithful* along was very reassuring. What a blessing, Lord, to have Charlie and Joyce along for friendship as well as assurance that we were not alone.

During our trip for the next several weeks with our friends, we took turns leading us through the Trent Severn Canal system in Canada. This was a wonderful 240 mile waterway with twenty-two locks, through a convoluted series of rivers, lakes, canals, and assorted streams from Trenton on the Canadian side of Lake Ontario to Lake Huron at Severn, Ontario. This waterway was completed in 1920. Before the canal was constructed, the waterway was used in support of the fur trading industry which required canoes and many portages, but was much shorter and not as challenging as the Great Lakes through Lake Huron, Lake St. Clair, Lake Erie, and Lake Ontario. The construction of this waterway was a very great challenge and was much delayed due to lack of funds, the Upper Canada Rebellion, and World War I. Although the original purpose of the waterway was commercial, by the time it was completed, ships had become too large, and railroads had been constructed that transported most of the freight. The use of the canal, however, became a major recreation attraction, perfectly positioned as a cruising area for local and transient boating. Development along the canal and its islands has created a thriving recreational economy, and a wonderful experience for boaters.

The eastern part of Lake Huron is extensively populated with thousands (and maybe millions) of rocks and islands all along the Canadian shoreline. There is a small-boat route marked out that allows passage without venturing out into the daunting Lake Huron with few bays or facilities for protection or supplies. The challenging part for us small-boaters was that the marker buoys were much smaller than we were used to in the U.S., and they were often very far apart, so visual navigation was intimidating. We alternated leading the way between *Empathy* and *Old Faithful*. One day, we missed a marker buoy and before we were aware of it, we were out into the greater Lake Huron. Looking back and faced with literally dozens of islands and rocks in sight, finding the small-boat channel was virtually impossible. It was too dangerous to just slowly make our way through the islands, as submerged rocks and fiberglass hulls are not compatible. As we explored the possibilities, I noted a radio tower that was on the mainland. On the chart for the area, I was able to identify the tower and be able to determine a course into and alongside of an island, which we were able to navigate very carefully, back to the channel. Thank you, Lord, for helping us find our way!

Our plan was to meet our son, Jim, and his son, Spencer, and for him to bring his sailboat that is on a trailer. Also, our son Stan and his son Brian flew up from Phoenix, Arizona, to experience the "Grand Finality," the last hundred miles of our two-year adventure. This would give us one week, sailing two boats together with two of our kids and two grandkids. What a great joy with many memorable events. In order to give Jim some experience navigating, I had him plan and lead the flotilla. As we had been sailing in Canadian waters, we needed to check in to U.S. Customs at a marina on Drummond Island. That is a U.S. island just east of the Upper Peninsula of Michigan. Our plan was that after checking in with customs, we would take a short sail over to a beautiful anchorage in a bay in Harbor Island. Before launching out, I complimented Jim on his navigational skills, and that "I would follow him anywhere." By that time I was, obviously, very confident is his abilities and I did not check our route as it was a short sail to an island that we could see, around some smaller islands. Within fifteen minutes of departure as I was following him closely, he ran aground and stopped. My attention was distracted when it happened until Katie yelled to stop. We were so close that there was considerable anxiety about running up on Jim's boat, but we managed to avoid him. There was no damage except Jim's ego. He had picked a wrong way between two islands. Thank you, Lord, for saving us from damage!

The remainder of our Great Adventure north was uneventful. Katie and I were full of gratitude, Lord, for the joy of the journey, for safety and security, for keeping *Empathy* from damage, and for the thrill of experiencing your creation. The expression "Thank you, Lord" seems totally inadequate for our gratefulness.

For the beauty of the earth
For the beauty of the skies
For the love which from our birth
Over and around us lies.

Lord of all, to thee we raise
This our hymn of grateful praise.

For the beauty of each hour
Of the day and of the night.
Hill and vale, and tree and flower
Sun and moon, and stars of light.

For the joy of human love,
Brother, sister, parent, child,
Friends on earth, and friends above,
For all gentile thoughts and mild.

Lord of all, to thee we raise
This our hymn of grateful praise.

—Text by Folliot S Pierpoint, altered
Based on Ephesians 5:20

Chapter 15

SAILING THE NORTHERN WATERS

For the next two years, we sailed *Empathy* out of the Upper Peninsula, and sailed the U.S. and Canadian waters. The second summer, Jim drove up to Spanish, Ontario, to sail with us on our boat for a few days and visit the beautiful Benjamin Islands. Katie and I had been cruising through the North Channel for a few weeks, and in order to get to Spanish, we had to traverse through a very narrow waterway between two large islands called Little Detroit Narrows. The afternoon before we were to meet Jim, the motor would not start despite trying everything possible. I called Jim and had him bring up his motor for us to use the rest of the summer, as he was not planning to use it. The challenge that we had, however, was how we could get to Spanish through the narrow waterway by sailing, without a motor. As we approached the narrows, the wind dropped to near zero and what winds we had was off the bow. In addition, there was a current between the islands that was against us. Our dinghy motor was only a 3 ½ mph, barely strong enough to push the boat, and the opening was slightly too small for both of the motors to fit on the stern, and the main motor was much too heavy to bring it on board. By using a very small hand saw, I was able to cut into the corner of the opening, just enough to allow the dingy motor to fit into the opening, but there was not enough room to be able to turn the motor for maneuvering the boat. I discovered that the motor would drive the boat just fast enough for the rudder to control the boat direction, and we were barely able to proceed on to Spanish and dock the boat just before Jim arrived. Thank you, Lord, for helping us to devise a way out of our dilemma.

In exploring the many islands along the southeast coast of the Northern Peninsula, we came into Cedarville, a quaint small town where we wanted to stay overnight Saturday and attend church on Sunday. We came into a small marina that was about a mile from town. After tying up, we befriended a couple that was just heading out in their nice big power boat. After a chat, they learned that we had no transportation and that we expected to walk into town. He offered his brand-new Lincoln for us to use and enjoy the unusual features of the car, while they headed out for a weekend cruise. When we were done, he asked us to just leave the keys inside of the gas cover. It was a warm day, and we discovered an ice cream store that was a wonderful surprise. We asked the young lady that waited on us if she knew of a nice church where we could go the next day. She said yes there was one and explained how to get there. She also said that she was very familiar with it, as her father was the pastor. We did attend the next day, and it was a great experience. Thank you, Lord, for these blessings—especially the people who loaned us their new car, even though we were complete strangers!

Later in the summer, we were returning to the marina at DeTour Village and went into a wonderful sheltered bay on the corner of Drummond Island. We had anchored there twice before even though it was a challenge to get into due to numerous rocks around the entrance. We stayed the night, and the next day was to be our last for the season. As we came out and were away from the entranceway, we headed toward the lighthouse that was some distance away in open water. While we were raising the sails for the last time that season, suddenly the boat hit a rock. We backed away from the rock and continued with the sails. I noticed that there was a red flag there, but it just did not register that it was a warning flag out here in open waters. A few minutes later, Katie noticed that water was filling up the walkway in the cabin as we were taking on water. The electric bilge pump had not been hooked up, as it was very slow and not useful. I had a hand pump that was much faster, with the outlet that went out through a window. I went for the VHF radio to call the coast guard. Because the stations were some distance away, the only way to get good reception was to attach the radio to the connection on deck at the base of the mast. There were two coast guard stations, both of whom were about forty-five miles away, in different directions. I was able to contact them, but I then had to quickly return to bailing out the water. They kept calling me, but I was too busy to answer. Because of the distance, it would take them about thirty minutes to get to us. I was barely able to stay ahead of the incoming water, but it would be questionable that I could last until they arrived. Suddenly, a motorized inflatable dinghy arrived with three young men with pails and they jumped on board to help us. They had on matching T-shirts and were, apparently, a crew on a boat. I looked out and observed a sizable dark maroon powerboat where these young men were from. They were able to stay ahead of the incoming water where it only came up about four inches above the floor—not yet into the electronics. Soon, thereafter, two coast guard boats arrived with a total of seven men and immediately connected up a pump that would drain the water in a matter of about five minutes or less.

When the coast guard arrived, the young men started departing and I handed Katie a notebook and pen to get their names, etc. Later, after things settled down, I asked Katie about them, and she said that they politely declined to give out information on themselves. We never again saw the boat and have no information on it. I don't know how the Lord was able to do this rescue, with such perfect timing to save us and prevent complex damage to the boat, but I can only praise the Lord for saving us and our beloved *Empathy*.

The coast guard accompanied us to the town launching ramp and dock, but tying the boat to the dock did not solve the dilemma as water was still coming in. They would still have to come aboard periodically to pump us out. They explained that the situation was causing their leadership a problem, as their regulations stated clearly that their responsibilities ended when the rescued boat is secured to the dock. In jest, I offered to launch off again so that they could rescue us again to force their management to make a favorable decision. Also, they were having a problem determining where there was a haul-out facility for us to be taken out of the water. It was a beautiful, warm day and the cap that I was wearing at the time of the event dropped into the water in the boat. So, I went below and got my other cap, which was a bright red Ohio State University cap. As I brought it out of the cabin, knowing that the coast guard personnel would be Michigan fans, I joked as I put it on that I didn't mean to offend them, but it was the only dry one that I had. One of the men said, "I think that you would be better off putting on the wet one." During this entire event, neither Katie nor I had a moment of fear; we took it all in stride and had such good humor talking with the CG members.

After about forty-five minutes, instructions from the CG office came that they found a haul-out facility about a mile away, and they were authorized to accompany us there. We had to stop and get bailed out twice getting there, and upon arrival we could proceed directly into the lift and we were out of the water in minutes. We were hauled out, put on a cradle for storage, and were allowed to stay on the boat, hook up electrical power, and we were given keys for the bathroom and showers. The marina said that we could stay on the boat as long as we would like. Lord, what a testimony of your help in times of trouble, and how you brought us peace and joy, instead of fear and anxiety!

Before this event, Katie and I had already decided that we would sail only one more season before ending our sailing days. At the ages of seventy-eight, and after thirty-five years of sailing experiences, we felt that we had done it all and was time to have other adventures. The next summer, we repaired the damage to the keel, and we had invited all of our kids to come for their last sail on *Empathy*. Stan and Suzie, Jennifer, and Jim were there with his wife, Christan. We had a blessed time with the families. It was then that Stan introduced us to his iPhone, which had recently been developed, and to the GPS capability. It even showed us the weather in the DeTour Village area and showed that a storm was approaching us from the west, about twenty miles away. We then decided that we had time to take a one-hour sail and get back before the rain came, and we did. What an amazing device in those days. The next day, we all drove to Sault Ste. Marie to watch freighters be locked between the St. Mary's River and Lake Superior. At the end of the afternoon, we decided to have dinner out, but where? Stan asked, "What kind of food do you want to eat—Chinese?" We said yes, and he found four restaurants that were nearby, menus shown, and even rated by people who had eaten there. This was our first introduction to Google. Katie was not in favor of us ever having one, as she knew how frustrating new technology was for me to learn. Little did we know then that this technology would play a major role for us less than a year later. I suspect that the Lord knew all about the technology, and how much we would depend on it later the next year. Thank you, Lord, for the joy of having family celebrate our last sailing summer and to this new technology that man has just discovered.

At the end of the summer, Katie and I set sail to Cheboygan in the lower part of Michigan, near the Upper Peninsula. We then planned to take the boat out of the water and trailer it to the family cottage nearby. Just as we sailed by the big Mackinaw Bridge, linking the two parts of Michigan, to the west of the bridge was a beautiful rainbow. It was at that same time that we realized that our very first challenging sailing adventure thirty-five years before was sailing by this bridge. It was then that we were reminded that the beginning and end of our cruising adventures was in the same waters, that the Lord was helping us celebrate by displaying a rainbow. How remarkable. Thank you, Lord! Thus ended our thirty-five years of sailing adventures on *Empathy*.

Psalm 139 speaks to me so very much (excerpts with comments):

> O Lord, you have searched me and you know me.
> You discern my going out and my lying down.
> You have laid your hand on me.
> Where can I go from your Holy Spirit?

If I make my bed in the depths you have been
there for me.
If I settle on the far side of the sea, you have been
there for me.
If I say, "Surely the darkness will hide me," you
have been there for me.
I know that all the days of my life were written
in Your book before one of them ever came
to be.
How precious are your thoughts, O God! If I
were to count them, they would outnumber
the grains of sand.
When I awake, you are with me.
Search me, O God, and know my heart, test me
and know my anxious moments.
See if there is any offensive way in me, and lead
me in the way everlasting.

Help me, O Lord, to be all that you want me to be during my
remaining days. Help me also to adequately proclaim how I have
seen your involvement throughout my life and the adventures that
you have been with me.

Chapter 16

PERSONAL CARE MINISTRY

I seemed to have been born with a soft heart and a huge amount of compassion for others in need. I have always loved my family, my aunts and uncles, my grandparents, my Lord, for Katie, and for life itself. I was one who always wanted to please and was compliant with the desires of my parents and relatives. When I peddled newspapers, I always wanted to please my customers. I always enjoyed pleasing my teachers, even though I was not a serious student as I never expected to go to college or become anybody of distinction. I had fun in life, and my philosophy was that having social skills was every bit as important in adulthood as being smart and having an education. At the same time, as a youth I had confidence to seek opportunities—if someone asked for a volunteer, I would go for it without hesitation. As an example, when I was as a junior in high school, I joined the Civil Air Patrol (CAP) as a cadet and went flying as often as possible with adult members who had their own airplane. In addition to just flying with pilots, I helped organize search and rescue training missions, to help train members to be prepared for our primary mission, searching for downed aircraft, should the need arise. I was actively involved, even the year after high school graduation. I received a letter from the Ohio State Civil Air Patrol appointing me to participate in a one-month exchange program to Europe, all expenses paid. Unfortunately, I had to decline this invitation as I was entering West Point at the same time.

Throughout my adult life, I participated in every available church activity including playing piano/organ duets as a teenager, youth retreats, choir, Sunday school, and community outreach projects. Katie and I were always very active in each church that we were attending. At age fifty-five, when I realized that the Lord knew me personally, I became inspired to help others as the opportunity presented itself. When our friend, Day, discussed with me that in her apartment complex was a mother and father, Fatima and Kerite of Indian descent, with three children that had just come into this country and had no furniture, I was motivated to help. They had come from Tanzania and were allowed to bring only fifty dollars for each member of the family of five. I proceeded to enter a notice in our church bulletin, appealing for furniture donations. I then used my modified boat trailer to collect the items and delivered what was donated. The amazing thing was that enough furniture was donated to furnish every one of their needs, including bunk beds for the two boys. During this effort, Day discovered another family in her apartment complex that needed furniture, Rita and Ivan with a boy and a girl. Enough furniture was eventually donated to totally furnish both apartments with not one unneeded item, and then the donations stopped! Amazing how you did that, Lord! As I am writing this chapter about fifteen years later, both fathers have passed away. However, I continue to be friends with the rest of the family, to be helpful where I can, and to be an encourager. Both families have thrived, are active believers, and all of the children are grown and successful.

Katie too had a real heart for helping others. A couple in our Sunday school class, Richard (Rick) and Peggy, had an adopted daughter, Amy, who at that time was about twelve years old. We became very close friends, as Rick was a Naval Academy graduate, and we had much in common. Rick ended up contracting cancer and soon died. Within a year later, Peggy also ended up with breast cancer and, in time, was very seriously ill and in the hospital. When Peggy was released from the hospital, Katie invited her to come live with us indefinitely, while her daughter was placed into a Christian youth care facility in northern Florida. Peggy then sold her home and moved in with us. While she was living with us, she fought hard with all-natural alternative therapies. Her condition steadily improved, aided by Katie's good cooking and the loving friendship, and within a year, Peggy was able and interested in purchasing a condo nearby. This she did and was able to live by herself unaided, until her cancer came back and became terminal about two years later. For her final days, she arranged to go to Atlanta, Georgia, to a Catholic cancer facility run by nuns. This facility was devoted to providing tender loving care for terminal patients during their last days. In Peggy's case, it was about one month from arrival. During this end-of-life event, the Lord was clearly present in the final visit by our Sunday school class. On Sunday, a few days before Peggy went to Atlanta, we decided as a class to visit her at her condo in the afternoon. Our teacher and my good friend, Ernie, Katie, and I went over with about ten others for the visit. But…what are we going to say? We had no prior discussions or plans of any kind of what we would do or say as we would just "play it by ear." After we offered our greetings, Ernie suggested that we sing a hymn. After we sang, I talked about a funny incident in my life, and we then sang another hymn. Then Ernie would tell of a funny incident and then sing another hymn. We did this until we were all laughing along with Peggy as well. This went on for about forty-five minutes, we all had a joyous time, especially Peggy, and we were able to say our goodbyes with joy in our hearts. Thank you, Lord, for your orchestration, making a sad situation into a joyous event. Your presence was so very apparent!

A nephew, Roger, and daughter, Jennifer, living in New Orleans, lost their wife and mother, Lindy, to cancer. Soon thereafter, they decided to move to Tampa. When they came, we invited them to stay in our home while they found a home to settle in, and they stayed for about two months.

Back in 1993, I befriended a cousin, Jack, of Ernie's wife, Joyce. He was in a rehabilitation facility near Tampa Hospital, in final stages of cancer. I would go at least once each week to bring and share a lunch with him along a waterway nearby. He introduced me to information about God's all-natural antibiotic, colloidal silver (CS). To produce it was a simple process that could be accomplished at home. This product is made from distilled water in a sixteen-ounce glass, with two silver rods hanging inside the glass. A battery pack, using three AA batteries, was hooked to the silver rods, and in approximately one hour, the process is complete. The solution contains very tiny silver particles in suspension and is very effective against bacteria, fungus, viruses, skin illnesses and burns, mosquito bites, and the like. It acts just like the immune system, identifying and eliminating materials that are foreign to the body. Due to the instability of the voltage and the resulting silver particles providing a gray-colored solution, it did not appeal to me to consume it internally; I started experimenting with alternate ways to generate colloidal silver. In time, I found a plug-in wall transformer providing consistent DC voltage that would produce a solution with particles of silver that was so small as to be invisible. I found this much more appealing to ingest it, and I had it tested and found to have a concentration that met the criteria considered to be safe and effective. Unfortunately, Jack died soon thereafter, but I have continued to develop and use what I refer to as God's all-natural antibiotic. Silver has been known for hundreds of years to have been helpful in maintaining good health, I have now been using this colloidal silver (CS) for over twenty-five years, and my health is about as perfect as it could be at age eighty-four.

Once I became confident on the healing powers of CS, I began experimenting it with others. Soon after developing it, I pursued whoever the Lord led me to that needed his antibiotic. I never promoted it in any way, as I knew that the American Medical Association (AMA) would not take kindly to "practicing medicine without a license." The Lord did bring me to two people who had acquired immunodeficiency syndrome (AIDS). This occurred nearly twenty-five years ago, and I really cannot recall how I was introduced to them. Both of them were in the dying stage of their illness. The first person that I was introduced was Robin. She was so sick from AIDS that she had lesions all over her body and unable to sleep. This was contracted through a blood transfusion, as this was early in the medical understanding of the disease, and a requirement of screening blood donations for AIDS had not been imposed. I was able to provide her with a generator where she could produce her own CS, and she got on it with my recommended full dosage. About ten days later, she called me all excited, as she had experienced considerable improvement in her diabetes, and her lesions had disappeared. And now, over twenty-five years later, she is still alive. I have been a close friend, calling or visiting her at least every two weeks, even though she lives nearly an hour away from my home. I have encouraged her to remain faithful in her trust in our Lord, and he has been faithful to her prayers. She has prayed that she could live long enough to be with her grandchildren, and she now has three of them ages six, eleven, and sixteen. She has always been very disabled, with no transportation, and unable to attend church, but listens to a Christian TV station all day, every day. Recently, she has requested that I administer Communion with her periodically. I was able to borrow a nice Communion kit from my pastor, and it is available to me whenever I wish. The first time that we held Communion, she invited all three grandchildren and one of their deadbeat fathers, to be with her. During this service, I was inspired to ask the kids questions as to the meaning of what we were about to do. The nine-year old (at the time) girl anxiously answered all of my questions, as their mother had had them in Sunday school and church every Sunday.

Another individual that I became aware of with AIDS was Dallas. He was a friend of my son, Bob, as a working associate at an auto parts store. Soon after their friendship began, Dallas learned that he had the disease. At that time, the medical community had no effective treatment and he knew that he would soon die. As a result, he left Tampa to live a lifestyle that he thought would bring him enjoyment during his remaining days. He got tattoos, silver adornments, began drinking heavily, and whatever else he chose. He told a mutual friend, Lynn, where he was staying, several hundred miles away, but made him a promise not to tell anyone else. When I heard about Dallas, I insisted that Lynn give me his address, which he finally did, and I sent Dallas a CS generator with instructions of how to use it. Dallas did use it, his condition kept improving, and here we are over twenty-five years later and he is still living. The interesting thing is that after he was feeling healed, he got complacent and got off CS. In time, the AIDS virus came back with a vengeance, and he had to fight it off again. He has copies of the medical reports on his tests through the years, showing these conditions. By now, his blood test shows that the virus is no longer even in his DNA, as it was before. During all of this, he has become a believer and knows who the Great Healer is and is volunteering his time at a church food bank.

Over twenty years ago, my friend, Lisa, was aware that I had a genuine heart for helping others, and she introduced me to Gwen who lived nearby and had a ministry in her home, caring for elderly women. When I met this wonderful soft-spoken lady, who had four residents, she explained how she came to her ministry. She had contracted the lupus illness that at the time had no cure. It is a very painful autoimmune disease that affects many parts of the body. When she contracted it, she had a two-year-old boy. Soon after contracting her illness, her husband couldn't handle it and proceeded to divorce her. The progression of the disease was very rapid, the pain was excruciating, and the prescriptions were not helping.

Finally, one Saturday Gwen was so desperate that she threw the pills down the toilet and cried out to the Lord that he a choice to either heal her or take her life. The next day, she called her husband and pleaded with him to take her for a ride, just to get out of the house. After having a friend keep her son, her husband did come and take her for a ride. For some reason, she wanted to ride to Clearwater. As they were driving in Clearwater, they passed a classic old home that was for sale, and that day was having an open-house, Gwen loved large old homes and she ordered him to stop for her to look at the house. She got out of the car and started walking in front of the car, as the house was across the road. As she was hanging on to the front of the car, she experienced a miraculously healing. She then started running toward the house yelling, "I've been healed!" over and over. She ran up the steps, into the house, and up the open stairway was a realtor showing the house to a prospective buyer. She ran up the steps still crying out of her healing, and the realtor just happened to be a good friend! The realtor excused the buyers and embraced Gwen. In the meantime, her husband just took off with the car and left her there. The realtor then took Gwen home. Gwen was so thankful for the healing that she committed herself to the Lord's calling, to create a ministry of providing care for elderly women in her home. She had been doing just that for a few years before I was introduced to her by Lisa. I was willing to do home repairs, as an off-hours ministry, so I would drop in when I had time to help with her needs. One morning I dropped by unannounced to check on her and, as usual, I just came in the front door while announcing myself. I immediately heard her calling for help. I came into a hallway and found her legs protruding through the ceiling from the attic. A folding ladder was there and I went up and helped her out of her dilemma. She had overstepped what little flooring there was in the attic. We jointly recognized that the Lord's timing for me to arrive just when she needed help was totally miraculous.

Several years later, Gwen found and purchased a beautiful old mansion about two hours away, at Arcadia, Florida. This was a large, two-story brick home with high ceilings and a flat roof, built in the 1920s. Katie and I had just taken a Sunday afternoon drive down to see her, as it had been some time since we had seen her. Gwen was again caring for three women, and also had her ailing uncle living there. We, of course, realized that she needed our kind of help, and we happened to have some spare time. Katie and I then spent the next month helping out and staying with her as she had a spare room. Upon returning home to Tampa, within two weeks a major hurricane, Hurricane Charlie, was headed for Tampa. As we watched for it on TV, it suddenly took a turn and headed for Ft. Meyers and then on toward Arcadia. As we were tracking it on TV and when as it got just outside of Arcadia, suddenly a tornado appeared on the south edge of town. I immediately called Gwen to get everyone in the hallway that we had talked about as being the safest place in the house, and then the phone went dead. That was late in the afternoon, and the next day Katie and I had planned to fly out to Ohio for a few weeks but decided to stay because of the storm. Knowing that Gwen, or her neighbors, would probably need help, we loaded our van with materials, including a large roll of plastic and a portable generator.

Very early the next morning, we headed for Arcadia. As we approached the town, we observed that the large water tower on the edge of town was lying on the ground, and there were so many trees across the roads that we could hardly make our way to Gwen's home.

When we arrived, she could not believe that we were actually there, as she thought that we were on the airplane going north. The first thing I did was to start up the portable generator—a small one that I purchased for our boat, *Empathy*. She had a very large refrigerator with lots of food, and we got that going first. Then she had another refrigerator in the garage that we also powered up. We ran extension cords up to the second-floor bedrooms, providing power for lights and fans at night. Gwen then apologetically asked if we could power the pump in the fish aquarium to save them, which I did. I then went up to the flat roof that, fortunately, I could get to through the full attic that had an opening directly on to the roof. When I got there, I found it had lead roofing, and about one-third of it had been peeled off by the tornado. I immediately got the roll of plastic and covered the exposed part of the roof and secured the edges before the afternoon rains came. Later, we realized that getting the roof covered, we saved the entire house, as there came very heavy rains that would have ruined everything. As it was, the hurricane was accompanied only by very light rain, none of which affected the house except a little moisture in the attic. Thank you, Lord, that I was able to get there in time to save the food, fish, and the house from water damage. Katie and I then spent the next month helping clean up the yard, as her property is about three acres with many trees. There was debris everywhere, and if we got it to the curb, the town would pick it up. Gwen refers to me as her angel, showing up just when she needs me. I now, as I write this book, realize that the Holy Spirit is the one responsible for having me being at the right place, at the right time. Hallelujah, thank you, Lord, that we were able to help her with her ministry in such a unique time and desperate situation, and saved the house from total destruction due to rain damage.

After nearly fourteen years, I had lost contact with Gwen as her phone numbers had changed, I had an occasion to go through Arcadia and confirmed that Gwen still lived there, but no one was at home at the time. I left a message to call me, which she did and were able to reestablish contact. Recently, after losing Katie, I picked up Bob's wife, Michele, and my granddaughter, Lauren, and we paid a visit to Gwen. Michele had never met Gwen before and Lauren was nine at the time. Gwen still has her only son with her who is not married, so she has no grandchildren. Lauren and Gwen bonded instantly and we had a wonderful time renewing our friendship and meeting her new husband. When we were ready to leave, Lauren said to Gwen, "Would you be my grandmother as I don't have one?"

Gwen said, "Of course. I don't have a grandchild either, and I would love to have you!"

As we were driving away, Lauren said to us, "I just can't help but cry, as I love her so much!" Thank you, Lord, for this touch to us all from the Holy Spirit.

And then there is Deb, who I have touched on in a previous chapter, describing my support years ago in rebuilding her home in the neighborhood from a fire. When I make a friendship, it is forever unless our interests drift apart. Although Deb moved to the Atlanta area nearly ten years ago, we still stay in touch. Last year, a hurricane was approaching the Tampa area, and I had returned from Ohio to be there, to not only prepare my house for the event, but to be there for other people that may need help. In the afternoon before the storm, forecasted to be a category 3 direct hit on Tampa, Bob called and said, "I know that you want to stay through the storm, but we are evacuating and going to Georgia, and you are welcome to come with us." So, an hour later I departed with them to places unknown.

As we were departing Tampa, I got the thought of calling Deb to see if we could stay with her. She was delighted to have us come but warned us that the house was a total mess since she had just moved the previous weekend and was unable to settle in as she had to teach school all that week. We were arriving Friday in the middle of the night, about two o'clock. As we were driving up, she called and said that the next morning she would have to be at the doctor's office when he opens at eight o'clock, as she thought that she had broken one of her wrists while moving furniture. When we arrived about two in the morning, she met us to help get us settled, and we found the house full of unopened boxes. There were beds available for all four of us that we could make up and sleep in. The next morning, the doctor confirmed that her wrist was cracked, and put a support on to hold it while it healed.

Bob and Michele started in the kitchen, putting shelf paper in place, and arranging dishes where Deb wanted them. Meanwhile, I hooked up the washer and dryer, and for the next three days we had a very good time helping Deb get settled. During this time, Lauren had a wonderful time with Deb's cocker spaniel, exploring the backyard that was about three acres, a swing set, a climbing tower, and lots of interesting rocks. In four days, we had a very memorable time, and we really helped Deb get settled. In the meantime, the hurricane had weakened significantly as it approached Tampa, and there was no damage to either of our homes. Lord, what a wonderful plan you had for us all, saving the Tampa area from a potential disaster, helping us have a wonderful experience with Deb, and at the same time helping her significantly. In addition, we had a great road trip with Lauren and me in the back seat playing computer solitaire and having quality time together.

I have previously discussed Lynda, whose home I helped prepare for the market in 2008. After her home sold, Lynda then moved into her mother's condo nearby and lived with her until her mother died at age 102. I have stayed in touch with her through the years, providing home repairs as needed, helping with her storage needs, and providing much encouragement. Lynda was Catholic and a member of a church nearby, but not consistent in her attendance. Through the years, I continued to encourage her spiritual walk with the Lord, of which she has been lukewarm. I am never "pushy" in my spiritual outreach to others, but just an encourager, and praying for the Lord's work and timing to take place. The loss of her mother took a toll on her, and she decided to move to Atlanta to be near her daughter and family. She rented a large moving truck, hired men to load her belongings, and I drove the truck to Georgia where she settled into a very nice condo on the third floor. This unit was within about a fifteen-minute drive to her daughter's home, who had a husband with two children. Unfortunately, her daughter had a very demanding job, traveled often, and her children were very active in school. Her husband's family lived nearby and they had been supporting the family. For Lynda, the next two years she made her feel like a "fish out of water," and her health deteriorated. The medical profession could not find a cause of her health challenges, despite a myriad of tests. This went on for months. She was very unhappy and considered it a mistake to have moved from Tampa. I flew up to be with her, to encourage her in her spiritual growth, and revive her spirit for music. She had her grand piano that she had not been playing. She was not active in a church, but I did encourage daily devotions, prayer, and Bible scriptural reading. I encouraged that she develop a daily routine, starting with always having a music channel playing her favorite songs and daily devotions along with Bible reading. I also encouraged her to developing the habit of having her first thought in the morning be to thank the Lord for her good night's sleep and the beginning of a new day with him in it. After several months, she suddenly called me to let me know that she would be spending a considerable amount of time at her daughter's home. Her daughter's job was requiring a considerable amount of travel overnight away from home. Her daughter invited Lynda to stay in their home and to help provide for needs of her family. Her husband also traveled some in his job, so Lynda was filling in with the children. Lynda's demeanor changed considerably as she had become very happy to meet the family needs, and her health concerns mysteriously disappeared.

In addition, soon thereafter, her son in Minneapolis called. He had seriously injured his neck in an accident and, at that time, was also experiencing marital problems and his wife was not there for him. Lynda then rushed out to help her son and their two children. Suddenly, Lynda had another purpose in her life, and she became more joyous than I have ever seen her in the ten years that I have known her. Thank you, Lord, for obviously being involved in all of their circumstances, thereby bringing Lynda into a joyous life by feeling needed by her families, thereby taking her mind off from herself and that, in turn, has improved her health. She is realizing that the Lord, indeed, is active in her life.

In a previous chapter, I discussed the help and friendship I have enjoyed with Carol and Jerry. This year, they needed their wooden fences in the backyard replaced. I have struggled to keep the fences useful for years, but they now require replacement. They received a quotation for $5,500 to replace the back and two side fences. This amount was prohibitive for them, so I took the project on for the cost of materials. After a little over two weeks of effort, somewhat interrupted by other events, the finished results ended up costing less than five hundred dollars, and they even paid me for some of my efforts. The amazing part is what the Lord did. Behind the rear fence is a creek with the bank about ten out from the fence. The county comes along about every two years and cuts the weeds back. These weeds were going to be a nuance for me to work in. The morning that I started the installation of the replacement fences, I heard a piece of equipment on our side of the creek about two houses down. It turned out that the county just "happened" to be cutting these weeds, and by early that very afternoon, they had completed the part that was along behind Jerry's fence. Lord, your timing is incredible in bringing this cleanup at a perfect time to help ease this project.

As I am now writing this chapter, about a year and a half ago, I joined a Bible study group led by a very good friend at church, Lisa. They were reviewing a small book regarding "Finding Your Purpose in Life," which applied to me as I was doing many things but none with a realization that it was my purpose. This group has consisted of anywhere up to fourteen people. During the sharing time for prayer needs, one of the members, Gail, asked for prayers in coping with her depression. She had to finally divorce her husband five years prior due to severe alcohol and abuse issues. He had lost his job several years prior, could not get a job at that time, and reverted to alcohol. His excessive drinking led to verbal and physical abuse to Gail. Finally, after several years, she could not take it any longer. Even after five years following the divorce, she was still depressed. This was partly due to a traumatic head injury after her divorce, during her time as a school teacher about three years ago. She had obtained a master's degree in Special Education, but because of the head injury, she could no longer continue teaching. Instead, she was working in her own landscape maintenance business, which really was her passion.

She had recently been diagnosed as having post-traumatic stress disorder (PTSD) and was being seriously affected by the change of depression medications. Her demeanor was like a dog that had been beaten for a long time—obviously severely depressed. The next day,

I called her to begin to provide support in the way of encouragement—something that I often do when the Lord brings someone similar in my life. She was very appreciative of my call. Typically, I would call again in a day or two to offer scripture as a way of encouragement from the Lord. Gail was, and is, a very soft-spoken individual who welcomed my discussions, so I continued. As time went by, she seemed to be coming out of her depression. In June of that year about four months later I, again, traveled north to spend most of the summer out of Florida. About that time, she told me that she no longer had depression medication available as her insurance coverage had disallowed payment. This alarmed me, so I would call her every day for a few weeks, until she seemed to be coping okay.

About that time, in mid-June, I planned on launching my sailboat, *Empathy*, and keep it in the marina for two weeks. After losing Katie, I decided not to sell it, but keep it stored on the trailer at the family cottage. The year after Katie's departure, I launched it and lived on it in the marina for two weeks. This was pure delight, with all of the amenities available. This year, however, the weather was rainy and cold, was not pleasant in the marina, so I just stayed in the boat for two weeks. I decided that while I was restricted to the boat during this unpleasant weather, I might just as well refurbish the inside of the boat. We had owned and used it significantly for thirty-eight years, and it could use a lot of tender loving care. So, I proceeded to clean, paint, oil the teak, and accomplish repairs that I had prolonged for years. At the same time, I would call and talk with Gail at least every two days—just to do life together. After the two weeks were up, I realized that I had not once been lonely myself, even having been restricted to such close quarters. So, the encouragement that I was giving to Gail had an equal effect on my situation of being alone. Our relationship has now continued since then for over a year, with an understanding that this is a friendship and not a more personal relationship. I'm old enough to be her father. In the meantime, she has developed confidence in herself and her walk with the Lord. Since her divorce, she has been faithful in her participation in the Al Anon support group, and she now is able to counsel others that are struggling having been a victim of spousal abuse from drugs or alcohol. The Lord is so good at placing people together in such a way that it benefits each other, while he helps us to grow in our relationship with him and service to others.

The above examples are just a sampling of the many individuals that Katie and I have reached out to through the years. Through all of the financial challenges that I have experienced, the Lord has always provided. What loans that were needed, he always provided the funds to never miss a payment, or even be late. My credit has always been perfect. When I have been without income, I have never applied for government unemployment benefits—even when I was unemployed for eleven months. My commitment to my Lord was that he has promised to provide all of my needs, and I will faithfully seek and wait for his provision. If I accepted compensation from the government, I would then be beholden to it, and I have never wanted that.

In response to my quest to find my purpose in life, I have discovered that my passion is in serving the Lord one day at a time. He will determine my future and my purpose as time goes by. I am so motivated by him that I don't have to restrict myself in any way, as he keeps me inspired, joyful at all times, and full of a sense of usefulness.

> I'll say yes Lord yes, to Your will and to Your way,
> I'll say yes Lord, I will trust You and obey.
> When Your Spirit speaks to me, with my whole
> heart I'll agree,
> And my answer will be yes Lord yes!
>
> I'll go where You want me to go, yes I'll do what
> You want me to do,
> Yes, I will be what You want me to be, just tell me
> Lord, I will wait.
>
> —Kevin Lever

Chapter 17

A YEAR OF TRANSITION

The last sailing trip in 2014 was the same month that Katie turned eighty, and only two months before I did in October. That was about the time when I had to terminate my house painting and home repair business due to my knees objecting to any more of such abuse.

Through all of our fifty-seven years of marriage, our love for each other amazingly continued to blossom. At Valentine's Day, I got a bunch of heart stickers that I distributed all over the kitchen, bedroom, and the bathrooms, usually in obscure places. To this day, over three years later, I still find them—in the shower, on the toilet paper holder, on the backside of a kitchen cupboard, on the inside edge of the refrigerator. I have found a note that I had posted to Katie recently:

> My dear: I *really* appreciate you for helping provide
> for our good health, starting with approximately:
>
> 358 days per year
> × 3 meals per day
> = 1,095 meals per year
> × 57 years of marriage
> Equals—58, 615 meals!
>
> Wow! How can I thank you?
>
> Your ever-lovin'

There was a thought that I had written and posted on the back side of our medicine cabinet: "Although our love is a personal thing, it radiates to all who know us."

Through the years, I had been drawing my own version of a smiling face and used it numerous times and occasions. And now, three years after losing my dear bride, I just found one under the bed that I had placed on her pillow when she came to bed one night.

When it comes to Christmas gift-giving for Katie, I would not just run out to buy something that I thought the she would like. Instead, starting a few months ahead of time, I would be sensitive to any comment on what she would appreciate, or what I would be inspired about a gift. The Lord would never fail me. This year, 2014, as I approached the season, nothing seemed to come to mind. I would pray about it. In my weekly Bible study group, about two weeks before Christmas I discussed this dilemma with my friends and added it to our prayer time. When it came to Christmas Eve I was still without an inspiration, without a gift, and was in earnest prayer, when the Lord gave me an answer in my thoughts, "Remind her of the true meaning of Christmas—my Son." The next day after all of the other gifts were opened, in tears I told Katie that I did not have a gift for her other than the message given to me in prayer. Of course, none of us knew what this would really mean in the coming year. But, as the year played out and she was taken home by the Lord, I came to realize that nothing that I might have given Katie would have any value except Jesus in her life. Thank you, Lord, for the most precious gift ever given, and demonstrating that her going home to you was, of course, no surprise to you as it was in your plan for her.

In February the next year, Katie's older brother, Richard Clark in Eugene, Oregon, died without expectation. He was ninety at the time and had never been seriously sick. Katie and I both flew out for his funeral, and it was a typical Oregon February day, rainy and cold. When we came home, Katie had contracted a minor cough and some congestion—nothing significant. As time went by, these symptoms continued, but her doctor was not concerned as he was convinced that it was not symptoms of pneumonias or anything serious. Finally, in mid-May, I said that this condition was lingering too long, and her doctor ordered X-rays after which he was convinced, again, that it was not pneumonia. I wanted a second opinion and went to a doctor that had an office adjacent to our new, local hospital. We took a copy of the X-rays with us. After studying the X-rays, he said that he was walking Katie directly to the hospital next door and admitted her. He had detected a blood clot in one of the lungs, and he ordered further testing and treatment right away. More tests and X-rays were administrated from which it was concluded that she not only had the blood clot but also pneumonia was detected in the left lung, and there was some type of mass behind the pneumonia. As a result, Katie was transported to the main hospital toward the center of Tampa, where they had the capability of treating these illnesses. It took about a month to get the pneumonia under control, which was necessary before they could address the mass behind it.

For my birthday the previous October, our son, Stan, purchased and gave me a new iPad, which was nice to have but not necessary. Katie was opposed to any new technology for me, for she had observed the frustration that I had gone through with computers and laptops, so was not happy about it. I found, however, that the Apple technology was much more user-friendly than the Microsoft technology that I had experience before. When she was suddenly in the hospital, many of our family and friends wanted timely updates on her condition. I, therefore, started using email, but I didn't know how to develop a group mailing addresses, so I would have to manually type in all the addresses each time. The use of email helped me significantly as, otherwise, I would have to spend each evening making phone calls after being with Katie all day. However, soon I had a list of nearly twenty-five addresses that I would have to enter manually, for each message. In frustration, I finally told my daughter-in-law, Michele, to get with Stan's wife, Suzie, and figure out how to develop a group of mailing addresses that I can call up and use for the updates. After they did so, I could compose an update each afternoon, send it out before dinner with Katie in the hospital. After dinner, we would get into Netflix, in the iPad, and select a movie that Katie could watch until bedtime, while I went home to do whatever needed to be done. This iPad became a huge blessing and having it available when we needed it was another indication of the Lord knowing what we needed before we knew that we needed it. Multiple thanks to you, again, Lord, and to you, Stan!

As the pneumonia was in remission, the mass was then explored. The results were confirmed and announced to us by an oncologist, that Katie had stage 4 lung cancer, and it was incurable. What a shock! After the doctor left, a song came to mind immediately and I brought it up in Google on the iPad:

One Day at a Time, Sweet Jesus

One day at a time sweet Jesus
That's all I'm asking from you.
Just give me the strength
To do every day what I have to do.
Yesterday's gone sweet Jesus
And tomorrow may never be mine.
Lord help me today, show me the way
One day at a time.

I'm only human, I'm just a woman.
Help me believe in what I could be
And all that I am.
Show me the stairway, I have to climb.
Lord for my sake, teach me to take
One day at a time.

—Lynda Randle

(Google the title and listen to Lynda Randle sing it.)

Katie and I lay on the bed singing this song, praying and crying, knowing the seriousness of the news. Katie had previously declared that she did not want to prolong any illness, no life support. But, of course, we would explore other options that the Lord might lead us to.

Prior to this event by probable eight to ten years, a good friend of hers and fellow teacher at the day school, Mary, was dying of cancer. She discovered a unique hospital in San Diego, California, that provided alternative treatments to cancer victims. Mary applied and was accepted with the understanding that someone had to accompany her and be with her to help with her care, and Katie was the first volunteer. As time and treatments went by, Mary experienced remission and was eventually healed of her cancer. We were convinced that this was the place for Katie to go, City of Hope, even though Katie had chosen not to get the typical cancer treatments that would just prolong suffering. We sent her medical records out for their review, and we were convinced that they would accept her for treatment.

One other issue that we were struggling with was that we had subscribed to an HMO for our health care insurance in lieu of Medicare, as it offered some additional benefits over just the basic coverage. What we didn't realize was that it was a Florida-only insurance program without coverage in other states other than for emergencies, and she was about to peak out over the approved payments, as there was a ceiling to the approved coverage costs. Stan's wife, Suzie, took this issue on with an insurance representative that she was led to and determined that the best approach was to opt out of the HMO plan and revert to Medicare. The only problem was that this could only normally be accomplished at the end of the calendar year. Since this HMO was a Florida-only plan, we could technically trigger an immediate change into Medicare by moving out of the State of Florida. Under the circumstances, we agreed to come and move in with Stan and Suzie in Colorado, awaiting acceptance by City of Hope. When Katie was released from the hospital, we packed up to move immediately. We still had not heard from the California hospital, City of Hope, but booked a flight to Colorado awaiting their decision. The afternoon before flying out, City of Hope called us and said that there is nothing that they could do, considering her condition, that other cancer facilities couldn't do. We had no choice, however, but to fly out to Colorado to trigger Medicare coverage due to the medical costs yet remaining.

On the way to Denver, as I browsed the Southwest Airlines magazine, an article caught my attention. The article described an advisory program of nurses that could be consulted to discuss the medical needs that you might have, for them to advise the best treatment facility available for the condition. This was exactly what we needed, as we were coming to Denver, not knowing where to go and what to do for Katie. When we got to Stan and Suzie's home, she informed us that the next morning she had arranged for a nurse that she had heard of who will do a telephone interview with Katie and advise us where to go for treatment. Suzie had not heard of the program that I had seen in the magazine, but the telephone interview had already been arranged. As it turned out, this nurse was a part of the program that was described in the magazine. The nurse's advice was to go to the National Jewish Hospital, and she made the appointment for the next morning. At the hospital, our appointment was with the chief oncologist. Their program would consist of five outpatient treatments, one week apart. She explained that what made their program so unique was that there would be *no* side effects from their treatments—no nausea, no hair falling out, or fatigue. If there were any side effects, they would want to know about it immediately so as to treat it.

As this scenario played out, we found out that this hospital was rated as the best hospital in the country for lung cancer. In addition, the chief oncologist had been recognized by the State of Colorado, as the #1 oncologist in the state for three years in a row. In discussions with friends in Tampa, we found out that our Sunday school class was fasting for Katie each Friday. With all of these events that the Lord was orchestrating, along with the army of prayer worriers through the email list that had surrounded Katie's struggle, how could we help but be convinced that the Lord would being healing to her. I had seriously reviewed Bible scripture that supported healing, underlined each promise, and made note that I was declaring it for Katie.

The first treatment was on a Thursday, and it was "a piece of cake." During the treatment, she struck up a conversation with another lady getting treated, and we were invited to their home for dinner sometime in the future. Everything was going as if Katie was being blessed in so many ways. As I have been born an optimist as well as an encourager, I had no doubt that my dear Katie would be healed and be with me for some time yet. And then…

The following Monday morning, I woke up as normal about seven o'clock, and checked that Katie was breathing comfortably and was just sleeping in. By nine o'clock, I went in to awaken her, and I could not arouse her; she was breathing but unresponsive. We called 911 to take her to the hospital in Denver, some forty-five minutes away. On the way as I was riding in the passenger seat of the ambulance, I questioned the driver that we were going to the National Jewish Hospital weren't we, and he replied no, we are going to the Swedish Hospital as they had a much more capable emergency room. Who was I to argue? When we arrived, Katie was rushed into the ER, and I was offered a chair against the room next to her. Within ten minutes of arrival, her heart stopped completely. The medical attendance looked at me for a decision as to what to do, and I directed them to revive her. I did so, as opposed to Katie's medical directive, for a couple of reasons. Stan and Suzie were in Phoenix, Jim had come out from Michigan to be with us while they were gone, and Jenny was coming out from Connecticut the next day. I felt that it was important for all of us to be able to say our "goodbyes" to their beloved wife and mother before she was gone. The medical staff was able to revive Katie and put her on life support until such time as we gave the okay to take her off. The amazing thing was that the ER staff had name tags that showed that they were from the National Jewish Hospital—how could that be? To this day, only the Lord knows.

The next day, everyone arrived in the afternoon. The chief oncologist that had treated her came from the National Jewish Hospital, spent nearly an hour reviewing the records, and then called us all together. She stated that she had never experienced such an event before in her twenty years of experience. Her conclusion was that Katie had experienced throat congestion coupled with her light breathing at night, prevented sufficient oxygen from coming in and carbon dioxide being eliminated, and resulted in her systems shutting down—she went painlessly and without a struggle. Totally at peace! That evening, we all were able to say our final words to Katie, and then her life was allowed to go naturally. What an abrupt change of events. Katie's wishes were to be cremated, as there would be reason to have a memorial service for her in Tampa, and another service in Fayette, Ohio, where we had a burial plot in their cemetery.

I stayed on in Denver for another week before returning to Tampa, completing details. This also gave me time alone to process these unexpected circumstances. I had, literally, hundreds of people praying for Katie and I had read, underlined, and proclaimed dozens of passages in scripture promising her healing. The Lord was silent, of course, as he never replies to the question: why, Lord? She had never been in the hospital except to deliver children. She had no prescriptions. Her weight was within five pounds of her high school graduation weight. She bicycled, canoed, sailed, and walked consistently. Her faith was extremely strong, and she loved family, friends, her Lord, and life itself. She was my high school sweetheart, and we had a loving, adventurous married life throughout fifty-eight years plus six years of courtship. What a blessing, and what a loss for me and all who knew her.

What did come to mind was that, despite all that the medical profession could do, the Lord would take her when he determined that her time had come—nothing could prevent it! She was in his promised presence, with him in heaven where she knew she would go. He blessed her with ending her life without any pain and suffering. The only conclusion for me was that she received her reward for eternity, that he had clearly taken her, and it was all about me—my passion for serving him. I believed immediately that he was freeing me up to develop a closer walk with him. In other words, he wanted me to be unencumbered in developing a personal and deep relationship with him. I was convinced that he had plans for me every day until he took me to his home. At that time, I pledged to him that I wanted to work for him 24-7, doing whatever he wanted me to do. I have always been encouraged to have a strong compassion and empathy for whoever the Lord puts in my life, and I have lived with such a conviction, especially for the previous twenty years. My nature and desire was not to waste a day of my life, so I persisted with a positive, optimistic attitude, starting within two days of losing my dear Katie.

When I arrived back to Tampa, I met with Sherrie, a staff member of the Van Dyke Methodist Church who helps coordinate memorial arrangements. She made it clear that I would have complete freedom to organize the service as I wanted, and she would make it happen. Sherrie was already a very good friend of ours. I asked that our pastor conduct the service, at the end of which he would offer Communion to all, as Katie loved the tradition of Communion as often as possible. Interesting enough, for the next month, every church service that I attended offered Communion without prompting. I also asked that a keyboard be available for me to play during the service. I played and encouraged the congregants to join in singing:

> Precious Lord, take her hand, lead her on, help
>   her stand,
> She is tired, she is weak, she is worn;
> Thro' the storms, thro' the night, lead her on to
>   the light,
> Take her hand, Precious Lord, lead her home.
>
> When my way grows drear, Precious Lord, linger
>   near,
> When my life is almost gone;
> Hear my cry, hear my call, hold my hand lest I fall,
> Take my hand, Precious Lord, lead me home.

—Text by Thomas A. Dorsey
Music by George N. Allen

(I suggest that you Google "Precious Lord Take My Hand" and listen to Jim Reeves.)

I then played and led the congregation in:

> Because He lives, I can face tomorrow,
> Because He lives, all fear is gone.
> Because, I know He holds the future,
> And life is worth the living, just because He lives.
>
> God sent His Son, they called His, Jesus
> He came to love, heal and forgive;
> He lived and died to buy my pardon,
> An empty grave is there to prove my Savior lives.

And then one day, I'll cross the river,
I'll fight life's final war with pain,
And then as death gives way to victory,
I'll see the lights of glory and I'll know He lives!

Because He lives, I can face tomorrow,
Because He lives, all fear is gone,
Because, I know He holds the future,
And life is worth the living just because He lives

—Composed by Bill and Gloria Gaither

(Google and listen to the Gaither Vocal Band.)

Memories were expressed at the service by each of our children, followed by a reception dinner where others could share their comments about Katie—and many did as she was loved by so many. Two traits about Katie stood out:

1. Katie loved her family so much that she consistently sent greeting cards to them all, at each of their birthdays and major holidays, always arriving on time, never late. That was impressive, as she thought of them even ahead of time.
2. She had a wonderful lightheartedness, and sense of humor—off the wall sometimes. She blossomed in her two weekly Bible study groups, as they really showed their love for her and her love for the Lord. She was a friend to all who knew her.

It is amazing how the Lord shows his presence in such unusual ways. At the end of the reception in Tampa, a couple came over to me that I should know but couldn't remember their names. He turned out to be a distant cousin of mine, David, and his wife, Pat, that I had not seen in probable thirty years, and had no idea that they were living in Florida, on the east coast. As we were talking, David suddenly pointed to a box under the table and asked where I got that box. The name and address was a company in Ohio, about twenty miles from Fayette, where he had been general manager for several years, way in the past! Lord, you do such unusual things just to show that you are involved!

At an open house at Barb's home on the farm, a niece, Susan, presented me with a plaque that described my feelings with the loss of my dear Katie. She made this at her home after being inspired by my comments at the memorial service.

Special plaque that Susan made just for me

About two weeks later, I traveled to Ohio for another reception at my hometown Methodist Church in Fayette. The service and reception was similar to the one in Tampa, with a graveside service conducted by my brother, Elwyn, who is a lay minister.

A temporary marker was made and placed, marking the grave, until a permanent one was made and delivered. The marker said, "Katie's Resting Place." Along with the marker, I placed a very small little angel that Katie had had hanging from her car rearview mirror. I hadn't paid any attention to what was written on it at the time. I took a picture of the marker and posted it on Facebook. In a few days, our friend, Day, saw the picture and ask what was written on the little angel. When checking it, I was amazed to discover that it said, "Heavenly Angel, guide the way. Watch over my Angel each and every day."

Katie's temporary grave marker

Our friend, Day, had given me a sympathy card, and she had written the following:

> God saw she was getting tired, and a cure was
>   not to be.
> So He put His arms around her and whispered
>   "Come to Me,"

With tearful eyes we watched you, and saw you
    pass away.
Although we loved you dearly, we could not
    make you stay.

A golden heart stopped beating, Hard-working
    hands at rest.
God broke our hearts to prove to us, He only
    takes the best.

—Author Unknown

At each of the receptions, I had announced that in lieu of flowers, to contribute to a fund in Katie's name with Living in Faith, a ministry that our good friend, Russ, had established. These donations would be used to fund water purification systems for Cuba and Haiti. Sufficient donations did come in for two systems that were earmarked, one for each country.

I am sure that if Katie were able do so, she would proclaim:

When I come to the end of the day
And the sun has set for me
I want no rites in a gloom-filled room
Why cry for a soul set free?
Miss me a little, but not too long
And not with your head bowed low.
For this is a journey we all must take
And each must go alone.
It's all a part of the Maker's plan,
A step on the road to home.
When you are lonely and sick at heart,
Go to the friends we know
And bury your sorrows in doing good deeds
Miss me, but let me go.

—Author unknown

And this is my pledge now as I go forward without my beloved Katie: to cultivate friendships, to do good deeds as the Lord so directs, to encourage others in their individual struggles, to be faithful to him and be joyful at all times.

Chapter 18

KATIE'S LEGACY

Katie was born in 1934 to Charles and Helen Clark, residents of St. John, Michigan. She was fourth in the family of children, to parents who were active members of the Episcopal Church. She was baptized in the church, and she loved her consecration. She cherished the reverence of the service and was touched with the formality and devotion to the Lord that the service presented. She loved the *Book of Common Prayer* and the loving spirit that it provoked in her. She grew up in a very loving family, with her father a devoted, soft-spoken father and editor of the local newspaper. She loved the small town, about five thousand residents, and everything nearby where she could walk to school, to friend's homes, and to church. She loved her teachers, loved school and participated in numerous activities, and loved life itself. When she was about ten years old, her parents moved the family to Long Island, NY, when her father enlisted in the Navy, as he was devoted to his patriotic duty in WWII. After the war, her parents moved to Ann Arbor, Michigan, near her father's work as a writer for the Veterans of Foreign Wars (VFW) newspaper. When Katie was fifteen years old, her father passed away of a massive heart attack. At the time, Katie's siblings were in college, getting married, and various such circumstances. Her mother kept the home as long as she could, and when they had given up the home, the family went their various ways, and her mother joined the University of Michigan as a house-mother in a men's dormitory where she could reside.

At age sixteen then, Katie went back to St. Johns to live with friends of the family and to complete her senior year in high school. About that time, her sister, Barb, got married to Calvin Canfield and came to live on his family farm in Ohio. Cal was a pilot in the Navy Reserve, flying one weekend each month, while living on the family farm in Ohio. He was a graduate of Ohio State University, majoring in agriculture. The farm was about two hours away from Ann Arbor. Before Katie went to St. Johns, Barb invited Katie down to the farm for a weekend, to meet this "handsome farm hand." When she came to the farm, she came out to the field adjacent to the house to meet me. I was feeding corn to the pigs, and she came out in her brother's white shirt with the tails tied together around the waist. I gave her a ride on my tractor, and the rest is history. The invitation from Barb was written on two "penny postcards" at the time, as there was too much information to get on one. We double-dated with Barb and Cal and went dancing at an outdoor pavilion on nearby Hamilton Lake, Indiana. Lord, how little we realized the plan you had for us in the coming years!

Katie completed high school and enrolled in college at Ypsilanti, Michigan, to become a special-education teacher. Meanwhile, Barb's home on the farm became her home, where she spent holidays while residing in college. For the next six years, Katie and I saw each other occasionally but stayed in touch through letters—once or twice each week—as time went by. Despite the long-distance romance that developed, we were free to date others, if desired. Katie did date others on occasion, but I did not—I was smitten. In high school, I had a significant case of acne, and I was convinced that no one would want to date me, but Katie didn't seem to care about my condition. In retrospect, I believe that the Lord put us together. She loved me as my nature was similar to what her father had been, and she seemed to love me unconditionally. Our romance flourished! The year after graduation from Ypsilanti Teacher's College, she got a job in Summerville, New Jersey, to be near me for my last year at West Point. There was no doubt that her love letters through the years encouraged me greatly to press on with the challenge of completing West Point. I struggled very hard academically, as I was not a gifted academic student, but she emotionally kept me going. I did not want to fail her, and she loved to have an association with me and the academy. We were finally engaged, at the farm at Christmastime, and planned our wedding at West Point. We were married the day after my graduation, in the big Cadet Chapel where we exited under the swards of my younger cadet friends. Our reception was at the Officer's Club on base, a very memorable occasion despite the lack of money to afford anything elaborate. Afterward, one of Katie's uncles had remarked to his wife while driving home that he so enjoyed the experience at West Point so much that if he died on the way home, his life was now complete. The joy of finally being together after six years of courtship set a pace for our marriage that prevailed throughout our lives together. Our love definitely overpowered all of our struggles. Thank you, Lord, for our commitment to each other, and to you as well!

In my employment, I was assigned to the sales department, with my customers being the airlines located in Kansas City and west. I was, therefore, gone a great deal of the time. Katie, however, proceeded to make friends in the neighborhood. We bought a house in Sunrise Terrace, an ideal community on the outskirts of Binghamton, NY. The house had been built in the '30s, so we updated the kitchen; otherwise, the home remained as built. It had a half bath on the first floor, with four bedrooms on the second floor, a very small bathroom, and a walk-in unfinished attic. Each of our children, three of them at the time, had their own bedroom. Life was good, but hard to make friends as most of the neighbors were born and raised in the Binghamton area, and few of them had the exciting, traveling experiences that we had had. However, Katie endured and soon found some interesting folks in the neighborhood. When it came time for Halloween, Katie wanted a dress-up party with her friends and their spouses, and I was all for it. When they came, they were in costume, many with face masks, and I would welcome them, but I didn't know a soul, and was hard to recognize them later. We had great fun, as Katie knows how to make good friends, and this started a periodic gathering every few months, for years. It was always a covered-dish dinner, sharing our wives' delectables. We always stayed up late with lots of fun, and one friend, Fred, was great at the piano playing sing-able songs. This went on for over ten years, and we referred to our-selves as the Sunrise Terrorists. We joined the church choir in the Episcopal Church, joyfully raised the kids, learned to ski, and got into sailing. Lord, life was great!

Soon after locating to Binghamton, Katie became pregnant again and was pleased, as she always wanted a fourth child. Unfortunately, she had a miscarriage early in the pregnancy. Although she was very disappointed, she went on joyfully with life. When the kids were busy in school, she became a substitute teacher for elementary stu-dents. That challenged her, but her real passion was her family, to be home when they departed and to be there when they returned.

In order to get me mentally away on weekends from my stress-ful job, we would ski in the wintertime and got into water sports and camping in the summer. Katie would always prepare a picnic lunch for us, so that after work on Friday, we would eat while going off for the weekend. We did this so often, especially on three-day weekends that one weekend, for some reason, we stayed home, and we all remarked that it seemed very strange to be home. We loved being together to sail, ski, camp, canoe, and travel to Ohio on major holidays to visit our families.

A few years later, she became pregnant and delivered our fourth child, Robert (Bob), thirteen years behind Stan. What a blessing, and we have always considered that he kept us young and active through the coming years. Lord, what a joy Bob has been in our lives, and thank you for bringing us his wife Michele and then our dear grand-daughter Lauren.

In the eighteen years that I worked in Binghamton, I traveled extensively, especially internationally, as I was the customer support manager for thirteen years, serving all of the airlines, all over the U.S. as well as Canada, Europe, Africa, the Middle East, and India. Some of my traveling was extensive, and one project was in Ethiopia. I was there for about three months. Ethiopian Airlines felt so bad to take me away from home for so long, especially during the summer, that they said that if I could get my wife to England, they would give us passes to fly on their airline to wherever we wanted to go. Katie, therefore, was able to travel to Ethiopia, Kenya, Greece, Italy, France, and Germany. From there, Finnair gave me passes to bring her to Finland, where we stayed for a week before she returned home, and I went back to Ethiopia to finish the project. Thank you, Lord, for the opportunity to accompany Katie to such unique parts of your creation!

Another project that I had took me to Bombay, India. Air India also offered passes for Katie to come to Bombay, and from there up to New Delhi to see the Taj Mahal. When she returned home, the airline gave her a letter that authorized her to visit the cockpit of the Boeing 747. When she did, the captain got out of his seat and let her ride for a short time while flying over the western end of Turkey and into the eastern Mediterranean—a wonderful experience that she considered a blessing of a lifetime.

In the eighteen years that we were in Binghamton, every Thanksgiving or Christmas holiday was spent with Barb and Cal, either in Binghamton or on the farm in Ohio. The most memorable mental image that we had was Christmas Eve in Ohio. When we were there we would attend an Episcopal Church at midnight, about thirty miles away. We got out of the service about one o'clock in the morning, remember snow coming down on the way home. When we got to the farm, we would have eggnog while the kids were going to bed, and then starting the Christmas wrapping and arrangements around the tree. Their kids, Debbie and Jeff, were very young, and I remember spending a couple hours assembling a metal doll house and a complex farm scene for them, in addition to the toys for our kids. We would typically get to bed after three in the morning, and then the kids would get us up before seven. For Katie, she cherished these family memories.

One Christmas we purchased, as a gift to our family, a canoe from my brother in Lower Michigan who owned a marina. At the time, we owned a large Mercury station wagon with a roof rack. I thought that it would be easy to tie it upside down on top of the car, with plenty of room to store our gifts as a family of five. As it turned out, we needed more storage than the canoe would hold, and it was not easy to cover them up. The biggest challenge, however, was securing the canoe to the car. As we were traveling down the interstate highway, the canoe wanted to become airborne and lift off the roof of the car. Also, we had crosswinds and trucks passing by, which really challenged my ability to secure the load. Oh well, we made it thanks to you, Lord!

My many years in Binghamton were very stressful on me, and I was unhappy in my work. The company would not promote me to another position as there was no one who wanted my job, and management was very "political" when it came to company loyalty and associated promotions. I totally resisted the political game, as my philosophy was to judge me on the results of my responsibilities and not on whom I cultivated. Finally, an opportunity came up to join a company, Reflectone, in Tampa, Florida. They were interviewing and recruiting in Binghamton, and I jumped at the chance. After my interview, I was invited to a second interview, this one in Tampa.

For my second interview, Katie was invited to accompany me. The company had arranged a realtor to show homes to Katie while I was being interviewed. After my interview, I was invited to drop by on the way to the airport the next day while returning to New York. At that time, the company offered me a nice position and an attractive salary. When I came out to the car, I announced to Katie, "They offered me a salary that I could not turned down, and I think that I will never stop smiling again!" She immediately broke down crying, and didn't stop all the way to Binghamton. I was totally unprepared for this response, for when we were in the Air Force, we moved nine times in eight years, and she was always willing and ready to relocate. Two weeks later, I started my new job and she was left to endure the challenge of moving, after eighteen years in Binghamton. She had to pack up the household by herself, discarding much that we had accumulated along with the memories, and prepare the home for the market. When she arrived in Tampa, it was July, hot and very humid, and with lots of rain. But, she lovingly tried as best that she could, again making friends along the way. By then, we only had Bob at home who was going into fifth grade. Katie had extra time on her hands, so tried to sell Tupperware, without much success—her heart was just not in it. We joined a start-up Episcopal Church that was meeting in a storefront strip mall and immediately joined the choir.

The struggle that Katie had in selecting a house was she loved the old-style classic houses, and she found no charm in the cookie-cutter houses in Florida. After a long search to find the house that she was attracted to, we bought it on the spot as it had a beautiful view in the backyard. There were no fences, and the property was more extensive than most whereby no one could see in anyone else's house. The patio in the back, however, was a very small rectangular slab of concrete with no covering. I soon began gathering ideas and designed and built a redwood stained deck, overhead structure, and roof. The design was extensive, and I then explored where I could get the pressure-treated wood that I had seen in a magazine. I finally found the source, through Katie's brother in Oregon whose career was in wood products. He located a factory in Alabama that was just starting to expand in the East. When I contacted them, I was informed that they were not yet selling in Florida, but they would make a one-time shipment for the amount that I needed. In other words, I had to design, estimate, and order what was needed—one shipment only. This was number one-grade lumber, with no knots, and was guaranteed for forty-five years against termites and rot. When I received it, I found that it was pressure-treated so heavily I could not drive a nail in it without bending. As a result, I had to pre-drill for every nail. I built it totally by myself. My disabled neighbor would visit me every day to watch me construct it and said that it was built so well if there were to be a hurricane, he was coming over to live in my patio. This project helped settle Katie into being happier with her home.

Years later, she told me that if I ever considered moving, I would have to move the patio too. Katie was, even after two years, still not her usual happy self. One Friday, during our traditional TGIF cocktail hour, I said that I just could not stand her being unhappy, and that I would consider finding a job in the North if that is what she wanted to do. I also said that it was her decision, I would honor it, and she could take as long as she wanted to make the decision. A week later at the next TGIF time, she informed me that she had thought it over, and maybe it's not so bad here after all. The next day, Saturday, we went to the local landscape nursery and purchased $250 of plants, and that was the final breakthrough that Katie needed to revive her normal sparkling, jovial self. Years later, she said that that was one of the best decisions that she had ever made (next to marrying me). Thank you, Lord, for helping me be willing to sacrifice for her, and the change that you helped make in Katie. Years later, you will use this testimony in helping keep a friend's marriage together.

For over the next four years, we continued to attend the Episcopal Church. During that time, they built a large, brick church in a prestigious community nearby. We continued to be faithful attendees and choir members. Somehow, my spirit was showing me an emptiness and telling me that there was more to it than what we were experiencing. Finally, one day I announced that I felt something missing in my faith walk, and I was going to go elsewhere. I had seen a sign near home, announcing a Methodist church that was just down the road. I decided to go there the next Sunday, and Bob was interested in going as well. The church was new and had only been opened a few months. After the service as we were walking out, I turned to Bob and asked, "What do you think?"

He responded, "I think we have found a home, Dad."

There was a powerful spirit in that church that was very attractive—I had never felt it before. We attended a few more weeks and finally Katie said that she did not want to worship separately and started attending as well. We immediately joined the choir and were warmly welcomed by the choir director, Mary Jo, and the others. That began a whole new walk with the Lord.

We soon became members of the church. About a month later, it was announced that the church was opening a day school for pre-kindergarten children. Katie approached the staff and was soon employed as a teacher. She was thrilled to be with children of that age, and to be a teacher with an aid for about sixteen children. At that time, she was assigned a double-size classroom along with another class. Having that number of students in one room was very chaotic. I decided, therefore, to build a free-standing temporary wall that was insulated for sound, until a permanent wall was constructed a year later. Each side had its own entrance, so independence was thereby available. Katie fell in love with her kids, and they to her. She would come home bubbling over with enthusiasm, and the dinner table was always lively with stories about her kids. This cemented her joy of being in Florida and changed her life significantly. As usual, the Lord provided this opportunity for Katie, just at the time that she needed to heal the wounds of relocation. It was a perfect fit for her as it was a half-a-day job, she had flexibility to tailor her teaching to each individual student, and she developed a loving "family" in the bond with the children, parents, and coworkers. She had all of her holidays off, the summer was available to travel, and she had time to maintain a loving home without the stress of time constraints. She joyfully continued teaching for thirteen years.

What a huge blessing, Lord, and what a change you helped make in my dear Katie!

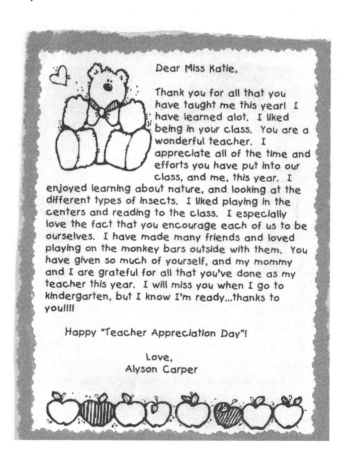

Dear Miss Katie,

Thank you for all that you have taught me this year! I have learned alot. I liked being in your class. You are a wonderful teacher. I appreciate all of the time and efforts you have put into our class, and me, this year. I enjoyed learning about nature, and looking at the different types of insects. I liked playing in the centers and reading to the class. I especially love the fact that you encourage each of us to be ourselves. I have made many friends and loved playing on the monkey bars outside with them. You have given so much of yourself, and my mommy and I are grateful for all that you've done as my teacher this year. I will miss you when I go to kindergarten, but I know I'm ready...thanks to you!!!!

Happy "Teacher Appreciation Day"!

Love,
Alyson Carper

Forever In Your Heart

Although you're not their parent
You care for them each day
You cuddle, sing and read to them
And watch them as they play.
You see each new accomplishment,
You help them grow and learn,
You understand their language,
You listen with concern.
They come to you for comfort,
And you kiss away their tears.
They proudly show their work to you,
You give the loudest cheers!

No, you are not their parent,
But your role is just as strong.
You nurture them and keep them safe
Though maybe not for long—
You know someday the time may come
When you will have to part,
But you know each child you cared for
Is forever in your heart!

~Author Unknown~

When Katie's mother became ninety-five years old, she was ready to stop traveling from family to family. When she retired from the University of Michigan, she packed her bags and started visiting her children and their families. She had no house to call home, so for the next thirty years she lived out of her suitcases. She would stay in each home for about three months, and then move on. She did this for thirty years! Travel was to and from their homes in Ohio, Oregon, California, and New York or later, Florida. This was not an easy situation as each home had its own challenge with relationships, especially with two women in the kitchen everywhere she went. She wanted to feel useful, and that was her interest in cooking. She endured it, but she felt that three months was about time to move on as she had her own strong personality to contend with. What she thrived on, however, was not only to be with her beloved children and their spouses, but she was able to establish a close bond with each one of her grandchildren, and they with her. They all loved Grandma Clark. When she turned ninety-five, she was ready to get off the travel routine, and Katie and I welcomed her warmly to Tampa, to make our home permanent for her. As all of our bedrooms were on the second floor, it was difficult for her to negotiate the stairs. So, we turned our dining room into a bedroom for her. We moved all of our furniture to the side, brought in a single bed, installed a folding door into the kitchen, and she settled in. The downstairs half-bath was four steps down off the family room, so it became difficult for her to negotiate, especially at night, as she had to walk through the front room and hallway to get there. I, therefore, built a very stable "throne" for accommodating a portable toilet and located it in the dining room the corner opposite her bed. For the remaining time that she was with us, I would dump it and refresh it each Saturday. This was very satisfactory for us all.

At the time that she was with us, I had an office and worked out of one of the upstairs bedrooms. In order to provide assistance to Mom Clark and relieve me to do my work, we hired a good friend, Day, to come and be with Mom each morning, until Katie got home from school. Day became a very close friend. She needed employment and companionship, so she was a real blessing for us all—thank you, Lord, for bringing Day into our lives. It is now over twenty years after Mom went to be with the Lord, and we are still very close friends even though Day is living one thousand miles away.

One of the problems for Mom during this time was having someone to talk with—especially on days when Day was not available. When Katie would return home from school after lunch, or when I would come down from my office, she would say, "Would you come in here and talk with me?" Her life was very lonely as she could no longer read, and she was not at all interested in watching TV. When I was working in my office, I always had a radio in the background, listening to Moody Christian Radio. Many of their programs were so good that I would tape them and play them again in the car when I traveled. So, loneliness in the office was not a problem for me. The challenge was how I could provide a similar capability for Mom, whereby she too could have her mind challenged. There were the physical limitations for her to turn the radio on and off, to tune the station, and adjust the volume. I got an idea and purchased a portable radio, opened it to clip the speaker wires, added an extension wire to a large volume control knob that I mounted on a beanbag. The radio went under the bed, always turned on and tuned to Moody Radio, and I positioned the beanbag and control knob on her nightstand. In that way, the radio was always on and she was able to find and adjust the volume from zero to whatever comfort level she desired at any time. When she woke up, she could lie in bed and listen to the news, music, and speakers that could stimulate her mind and keep her thoughts occupied. She could go to bed at night and listen to "Music in the Night" and go to sleep with soft music with the volume adjusted just as she wanted. Being an active Episcopalian all her life, she was not familiar with being "born again." However, after about six months of listening, I overheard a telephone conversation with her son in California, and Mom said, "Bob, I want you to know that I am now a 'real' Christian." I knew that it was her way of saying that she had asked the Lord into her life. And, what a difference that made in her nature during her remaining years! What an unusual way, Lord, of filling her life with joy during her last days!

One evening, when I went to visit her when she was going to bed, she mentioned that the previous night she had seen a vision of men coming in and out through her window, and it really frightened her. I said that what we need to do is to pray them away. I knelt down next to her bed, and I prayed for these demons to go away and stay away, and she never experienced them again. Thank you, Lord, for

217

making our home a safe sanctuary, where we can all be protected from the evil one!

Although Mom was with us for three years, we never felt that it was an imposition having her—it was our privilege to honor her in her waning days. Katie and I recognized that we made a good team; when one was "down," the other would fill in and be "up." We considered it a blessing. Thank you, Lord. It seems that in the last hours of our lives, the Lord often does something special. Mom eventually developed a serious pain in her stomach, and we took her to the hospital. She was never known to be an optimist, as she was usually anxious about things. I was in her room when the doctor came in to announce their findings. He informed her that she had a blockage in her stomach, and the only way to relieve it was an operation, but they needed her approval before proceeding. Mom's reply was, "That's okay. You gotta do what you gotta do." That evening when Katie was with us in her hospital room, we had the most pleasant conversation with her; she was totally at peace. As I walked out of the hospital with Katie that evening, I said, "This is the first day since I have known your mom, that I would have to categorize her as being an 'optimist.'" The next morning, the operation went well, but her blood pressure dropped low and never revived. The Lord took her painlessly. What a blessing, Lord, and this is the way that we all want to go!

In the last ten years of her life, Katie really seemed to blossom; she was so happy with her life. I attribute it to the fact that she really found happiness with herself. She joined two ladies' Bible study groups: one Monday afternoon at Tann's home, and one Friday mornings at Linda's house. Katie had an enthusiastic sense of humor, and her friends enjoyed her "off the wall" humor, and that reinforced her confidence in herself. I also learned, in later years, how joyous she was when I would devote undivided, quality time for her. This brought freshness to our already-devoted relationship, and a love "so divine." It was always amazing to us, how our love would continue to grow through the years, in new ways, different and better than ever before. She was definitely happy with herself, but most of all, happy with her love of the Lord.

Katie's "love language" was quality time. She loved to have uninterrupted time with her precious family and friends. She really enjoyed the sailing adventures, but the part that she cherished the most was the uninterrupted time on the boat, to be with her beloved captain and her loved ones. Our sailing trips to the Bahamas, and later up the Intracoastal waterway, was very special to her—no phones, no TV, no distractions, only time together. She wanted no part of making sailing decisions, especially what she needed to do during docking. But she was always ready to go again, and she had great confidence in me as her captain. Anytime her children or grandchildren could come sailing with us, she cherished, and she loved to write in the boat log of all of our adventures. She loved road trips as, again, it was uninterrupted time together. She *never* wanted the car radio on, as when she wanted to talk she didn't want to compete with it. I believe, in my heart of hearts, that our marriage was very stimulated with all of the trips that we planned together ahead of time, in anticipation of another memorable adventure. Sunday afternoons were not complete until we would go for a drive, to try to find a road that we had not traveled on before. This tradition continued to what turned out to be her very last Sunday at home. This travel spirit took us to every state in the union, including Alaska, except Hawaii.

I never remember a time when Katie complained about anything. She never wished for any luxuries; she was happy and very appreciative with what she had. One of the most cherished times that we had together was the second part of our fiftieth wedding anniversary celebration. When we came back from our cruise and visit to Alaska, we went to Phoenix and borrowed Stan's pop-up camper to explore the canyons of Utah and Arizona. We went on a two-week adventure, going from one canyon to another. We thoroughly enjoyed this time together, experiencing breathtaking beauty, with time not being significant. At the end of the two weeks, I commented that no American should die without seeing God's spectacular creations in the various canyons. Katie enjoyed the simple things of life: having our second cup of coffee in the morning outside the camper and watching a bird come up a take a drink of water from an open pot that was soaking. She had a great love for birds and always had a feeder outside of her kitchen window at home.

Katie's legacy is not complete without commenting on her devotion to her family. She always encouraged playing cards with her loved ones whenever we visited. All of the kids have laughed through "O Hell," kings on the corner, hearts, or gin rummy. We played cards at all of their homes, with Barb on the farm, at home with me or visitors, and especially on the boat during our travels. We would alternate evenings, playing cards or reading, and we never got bored with each other.

During Katie's last days in Colorado, she commented on how much she appreciated the uninterrupted time that I was having with her. She enjoyed me rubbing her feet or her back, to enjoy the beautiful Rocky Mountains together, to swing with me in the glider, to listen to my love songs and hymns that I would play on the piano just outside of the bedroom as we were going to bed at night, and first thing in the morning.

The Lord took her home suddenly, without any pain or suffering, and peacefully without any struggle. What a huge blessing she was to me, Lord, and I will forever be grateful for you putting Katie into my life.

> Time goes so fast, I thought it'd last, I never
> dreamed this day would come,
> Why are the years replaced with tears? Where do
> they all come from?
> Is Heaven the place you now call home? Does
> Jesus set and talk with you?
> I pray one day I'll hear God say that I can come
> there, too.
>
> I miss you so, but I will let go, because God has
> a plan for me.
> He needs me to stay until it's my day. Then I will
> finally be set free.

Help me remember all the times that we shared.
    Never let me forget your face.
God used your life to share His love and show the
    meaning of grace.

My heart still breaks and it always will. When I
    think back, I feel the pain.
God wants me to remember your life here on
    earth, and all the blessings that still remain.
I loved you yesterday, I love you today, and I will
    love you for all my tomorrows.
You are forever my place of Heaven here on
    earth, so I will look up and let go of all my
    sorrows.

—Sue Lucck Carlsom

Chapter 19

DEDICATION TO GOD
AND COUNTRY

For generations, both of our families have always had a deep dedication and appreciation of America's appeal to God in the foundation and maintenance of freedom and liberty. They also have been willing to serve in the defense of freedom, as they were called to do so.

The first to serve, as I know it, was my great-grandpa Vine, my mother's grandfather. He served with the Union forces in the Civil War and came home wounded in one of his legs. He had a limp for the rest of his life. Other than that, none of the other numerous members of our families ever lost their life or even was wounded. None of the below listed people ever saw battle where they killed anybody or destroyed things. This is amazing. Thank you, Lord, considering the number of people described below and the many years of service they represent. Although we served willingly, you kept us safe and out of harm's way!

Katie's father, Charles Clark, was a Navy officer in World War I and became the first military pilot in our long list of dedicated service men. He became a pilot toward the end of WWI, therefore did not see any action.

Katie's father, a Navy pilot

About twenty-five years later, he gave up being the editor of the St. John's Democrat newspaper in Michigan to enlist in WWII as a Navy officer. Although he had a family of four children at the time that could have given him a deferment exempting him from serving, his devotion to this great country inspired him to enlist again. He served in the Navy war room at Bennett Field on Long Island as an officer. During WWII, his son, Richard, became old enough to enter the Navy, and became a Grumman F6F Hellcat pilot, and was qualified to fly from aircraft carriers. He finished his training late in the war, too late to see combat. He did join the Navy Reserve and served for a few years after the war.

Cal Canfield, Katie's brother-in-law, Barb's husband and one of my mentors, went to the naval academy after graduating from high school. WWII was going on at that time, and after a year at the academy he resigned in order to join active duty forces. He went through naval flight training and received his wings as a multi-engine pilot, qualified in the Consolidated PBY Catalina, an American flying boat. This was an amphibious airplane used primarily for water rescue. By the time that Cal became qualified, the war ended. He then joined the Navy Air Reserve where he befriended Katie's brother, Richard. Richard had a sister, Barbara, who Cal then met and married—thus began the chain of events by the Lord, leading to Katie and me meeting and marrying.

As I have previously described in this book, I became an Air Force pilot after graduating from West Point. At that time, the Air Force Academy was not producing graduates, so 12 percent of West Point graduates could go into the Air Force. Upon my graduation from pilot training, because I had a conflict in my soul with having a mission of killing people and destroying things, I became an enthusiastic instructor in the Training Command. I then spent eight years total and flew, literally, all over the U.S. and three years in Europe. I primarily flew the Lockheed T-33 jet trainer, training new pilots, giving check-rides, and flying support missions.

And then along came our son, Stan, who was attracted to the academies. After a visit with our family to the Air Force Academy when he was fourteen, he decided to join it upon high school graduation, and subsequently was accepted. As an interesting sidelight, he had to graduate from high school, one of the first in line, so that we could rush him to the airport to meet his flight to Colorado Springs, CO, and be there for his reporting time the next day. His eyesight was not perfect, and he received contact lenses at the academy. When in his last year and evaluations were to be conducted for acceptance into pilot training after graduation, I encouraged him to try out. He had not been particularly interested before, and I suspect that was mostly because of his eyes. However, he took my suggestion, tested, and was accepted into pilot training upon graduation. This was clearly a miracle as he had been wearing contact lenses nearly all of his time at the academy, but they then tested twenty-twenty. The rest is his history, but in summary he was mostly an F-16 fighter pilot with the exception of a tour in the Training Command as an instructor, flying the T-38.

Stan and I with his F-16

He joined Southwest Airlines after a total of fourteen years in the Air Force. At that time he was a major with extensive flying experience all over the U.S., Norway, Japan, and Thailand. When he joined Southwest Airlines (SWA), he reverted to reserve status with the Air Force. Somehow, he got in touch with the academy and became a high school recruiter for the Phoenix area. That was not a paid position, but he could recruit as time permitted around his Southwest duties. For every year that he was a recruiter, he earned an equivalent year of active duty toward retirement. In addition to his flying duties with SWA and his recruiting activities, he somehow found time to get his master's degree. This qualified him for promotion to lieutenant colonel that, in turn, extended his authorized active duty time to twenty-eight years for retirement. He has now met his twenty-eight years and has also completed twenty years as a captain for SWA.

Stan in the Southwest Airline cockpit

Through all of the above active flying, the Lord has blessed us abundantly. None of these pilots ever flew in combat, never killed anyone or destroyed things, and never had a serious accident in all of the extensive flying hours accumulated. This miraculous record also needs to take in consideration that the aircraft flown varied from the very first military WWI aircraft, such as the SNJ, through the very first single-engine jet trainer, the T-33, the F-16 supersonic fighter, and the Boeing 737 passenger aircraft. The Lord clearly has watched over us all, for which we are supremely grateful!

Flyer's Prayer

When this life I'm in is done,
And at the gates I stand,
My hope is that I answer all
His questions on command.

I doubt He'll ask me of my fame,
Or all the things I knew, Instead,
He'll ask of rainbows sent
On rainy days I flew.

The hours logged, the status reached,
The ratings will not matter.
He'll ask me if I saw the rays
And how He made them scatter.

Or what about the droplets clear,
I spread across your screen?
And did you see the twinkling eyes.
Of student pilots keen?

The way your heart jumped in your chest,
That special solo day-
Did you take time to thank the ones
Who fell along the way?

Remember how the runway lights
Looked one night long ago
When you were lost and found your way,
And how-you still don't know?

How fast, how far, how much, how high?
He'll ask me not these things.
But did I take the time to watch
The Moonbeams wash my wings?

And did you see the patchwork fields,
And mountains I did mold;
The mirrored lakes and velvet hills
Of these did I behold?

The wind he flung along my wings,
On final almost stalled.
And did I know—it was His name,
That I so fearfully called?

And when the goals are reached at last,
When all the flying's done,
I'll answer Him with no regret-
Indeed, I had some fun.

So when these things are asked of me,
And I can reach no higher,
My prayer this day—His hand extends
To welcome home a Flyer.

—Patrick J. Phillips

Chapter 20

THE DEEPER WALK WITH THE LORD

A day or two after Katie was taken home with the Lord, I was convinced that he took her to free me up to develop a closer walk with him. At that time, I did not have scripture to support the fact that God would take a faithful believer, devoted and loving wife, one with no health concerns, perfect weight control, never in the hospital except for delivering babies, consistent exercise riding a bike, active with walking, sailing, canoeing, and with healthy eating habits. Why? Could it be to give Katie her reward in heaven and to free me up to do what my passion is in helping others? I didn't have any scripture to help me believe this, that she was taken home to free me up. Could it be for me, Lord? It was clear to me that the Lord had a plan for my life. I fully believe that this means every day of my life, and I never want to waste a day. So I went on doing the best that I could, day by day, with a positive attitude. I was reminded again of the song, "One Day at a Time Sweet Jesus"—that all I'm asking of you.

I have never allowed myself to get depressed or discouraged. I had my music ministry that I expanded somewhat, I had many people in my personal care ministry, I had many friends, and I had my church. In about three months, as we were approaching the Christmas holidays, our church had gone to a contemporary music format and the choir was minimized, without anthems, no special music, and no Christmas cantata. I decided to change churches and join with many of my old-time friends who, many years ago, started up a non-denominational church. This is where our longtime choir director, Mary Jo, and praise band were, and they were preparing for a Christmas cantata. I then joined the choir followed by joining the church, joining a Bible study group, and found myself surrounded by friends and activities. Life was as good as it could be, under the circumstances. Thank you, Lord, for leading me to Keystone Community Church, where I have again sensed your Holy Spirit so powerfully, and where I am growing in your grace.

In my many discussions with friends, I would often state that I was convinced that the Lord took Katie, but I did not have any scripture to support it. One morning, I called up my friend and neighbor, Sarah, and invited myself for coffee (I'm not shy). During our discussions, she told me that the previous evening, at her Bible study group, they were studying the book of Ezekiel and in the twenty-fourth chapter, God announced to Ezekiel that by sundown that evening he would take away the delight of his eyes (his wife). I then realized that scripture *did* provide a precedent for our God to take away the love of my life. I was greatly relieved that my belief could be true and supported by scripture. The very next day was Saturday, and out of the blue came a fax message from another friend, Linda— totally unrelated to my conversation with Sarah. The fax was a poem written by a noted evangelist, John Piper. The poem described how Ezekiel must have reacted to God's pronouncement. How he might have reluctantly announced it to his wife. And her reaction was joyful enthusiasm as Lord had shown her in a dream the previous night, how beautiful heaven was. Although she was sorry to be leaving him, she was going to where he had been preaching about, and how glorious it will be! What a miracle, Lord, to have these events occur in such a way as to help bring closure for me in my dilemma.

An interesting twist in my experience with the book of Ezekiel came about several years before. At church, our choir decided to have a talent show, where we could participate individually with our own talents and interests. I decided to dress up in a disguise and do a stand-up routine at the piano, playing and singing the song about Ezekiel called "Dry Bones." I was referred to as "Zeke" and, of course, for chuckles I mixed the bones up in the lyrics. After performing, I then took off my hairpiece so that everyone could see who I was. This went over so well that some of my friends still refer to me occasionally as Zeke. Katie was not aware that I was going to perform this routine and said later that she had no idea of who I was until she finally recognized my shirt. A few years later, we were at a Christian summer campground for a week with Stan's family. They also had a talent show one evening. I, again, did my Zeke act without the family knowing ahead of time. While I was performing, Stan was videotaping and, part way through, came to the realization of who I was. What an interesting set of circumstances that, of all the characters in the Bible, the Lord has given me an association with Ezekiel. As he did with Ezekiel, it was without explanation as to why. But future events reveal that he was causing us both to be available to him, unencumbered, to do his will unmarried. Wow—that's chilling.

Just before Katie got sick, I had put our boat, *Empathy*, up for sale on the Internet. Because I had higher-priority matters to contend with, I did not pursue any serious inquiries about the boat. The following summer, 2016, I decided to spend the summer out of Florida, as Katie and I had done for several years and to spend the time in the North and visit our kids. By then, I had decided to keep the boat and put it in the marina at Cheboygan, MI, for me to stay on for two weeks. *Empathy* makes a great bachelor pad with all the marina facilities available, my car for its freedom of travel, my brother Neil and his family living in the area, and Jim and Christan's boat in the adjacent marina. I felt that this would be a great place to start again on this book, as I already had written ten chapters prior to Katie's demise. I had a hard time, however, getting inspired. I had a dilemma anyway, as to how to end the book, as I know that my walk with the Lord will continue until he also takes me home. It was a delightful two weeks, but I never got back to the book. I then took *Empathy* out of the water and stored it back at the family cottage and decided that I would keep the boat for whatever the future beheld.

At the end of the year before Katie was taken, my knees were hurting badly, and I had to quit my house painting and home repair business. Toward the end of 2015, I had a few funds and decided to follow up on an article that I had found and saved from a Southwest Airlines magazine that described stem cell therapy for knees. I had not seen any other information about such a procedure, but it greatly interested me. The article was written by a doctor in North Miami. It was an outpatient procedure that sounded like a great possibility for me instead of knee replacements. I contacted him and made arrangements for treatments beginning in late November. The program consisted of a series of treatments, four of them for each knee, five to seven days apart. Since I was able to fly at no cost on Southwest Airlines, I would fly down to Ft. Laudable, FL, first thing in the morning and would then rent a car to drive about twenty-five miles to the clinic. After I got a treatment on each knee, which took about three hours, I would then drive back to the airport, turn in the car and fly back to Tampa—all in the same day—arriving about six in the evening. When I walked out of the clinic after each treatment, my knees would already feel somewhat better than when I went in. I was able to complete my treatment program before Christmas. The doctor informed me that healing would continue for at least six months and, although a "tune-up" could be available each year, he didn't expect to see me back for six or seven years. As I write this book 2 ½ years later, I have had no follow-on treatments, I have no pain, and I am able to return to some limited inside painting without any discomfort. I do not have endurance for long-distance walking, however, but I can ride my bicycle for miles without any complaints from my knees. Each day, I usually ride two miles, and on Sunday I could go typically ten miles, and still have no discomfort. What I really like about this therapy is that it uses all natural body substances, and relies on the Lord for healing through our normal healing process. Wow, thank you, Lord. It is only by your grace that I found out about this therapy and you have made the funds available to pay for these treatments.

From the donated funds from Katie's memorial services, two water purification systems could be funded—one for Cuba and one for Haiti—through the Living in Faith Ministry. My very good friend, Russ, founded this ministry twenty years before and developed the water purification system himself. About fifteen months after these memorial services, I was able to join with a group of thirteen other volunteers from Florida and various other states, for a weeklong missionary trip to Cuba. During this trip, we were able to install a total of fourteen systems. These systems are always installed in churches where purified water is needed, and the water is made available free for the neighborhood. This is used as an attraction for the neighbors to come to church, as an outreach to the community. Experience has shown that, within a year, the number of members at the church usually doubles. What a wonderful experience it was for each of us who went! One of the systems, in memory of Katie, was installed in a seminary in Havana, where there are approximately 350 students. A plaque was installed on the wall where all students are lined up approaching the cafeteria food service. The plaque proclaimed (in Spanish) that the system was in memory of Katie, in memory of parents of a niece of ours who were originally from Cuba, and the Living in Faith Ministry. In this way, the water purification systems could be promoted throughout Cuba through the awareness of the students.

At each church where we went, the system was installed by a plumber who lives in Cuba, with the help of two or three of us volunteers. At each church, a gathering of church members were always there to welcome us and to serve us an extensive meal, overflowing with "milk and honey." They were nearly all women, always standing along one side of the sanctuary as we entered. You can imagine how intimidating they must have felt with fourteen Americans invading their humble sanctuary. While the water system was being installed, which took about two hours, the rest of us would gather for a sharing time with these women. We had a very good translator with us, with a good sense of humor. During the discussions, I would always share that I was there in memory of my wife who was taken home by the Lord about fifteen months prior. I would then share that one of the things that I missed most with her gone were the hugs that we shared at least twice every day. I would then say that, because I missed these hugs, I would like a hug from each of them before we left. After a few of these visits, I then would go into a church and immediately go to the women gathered and hug each of them. Then later I would explain about missing hugs from my wife. In that way, it would immediately "break the ice" to get them more comfortable with us, and I would, thereby, get more hugs. By the end of our trip, I estimated that I had received over six hundred hugs, and I am sure that I left a lasting impression of the friendly Americans that came to their humble church. I came to realize that a hug is an international expression of love, and you don't have to know the language.

One of these installations was in a house church that had been started only a few years before. This was a house where the pastor and his wife lived in one side, and the other side was turned into a sanctuary that held about sixty people. When I was about to enter into our bus after the installation was complete, the translator stopped me and asked, "Do you see that little lady down the street that is standing outside of her house? She wants you to go down and give you a hug." The translator then explained that she had been in the church when I said that I had lost Katie to the Lord about fifteen months prior; she had apparently started crying and ran out of the church to her home. The story was that she had lost her husband five years prior, and she was still grieving. She apparently had a change of heart and got word to the translator that she wanted to give me a hug. I went down and got my hug from her. I do not speak Spanish, but I did point up and said, "Cristo amore you" (Christ loves you), "Ish amour you" (I) and "Amigos amour you" (friends). I got a big smile from her and another hug. Thank you, Lord, for this opportunity to leave a lasting impression on this lady, of your love, and I pray for you to provide emotional healing from her grieving.

Life has gone on in a positive way for me, continuing with my passions for music and empathy for others. As the summer of 2017 approached, I decided to continue with the tradition of leaving Florida for the summer. In May I learned that Katie's sister, Barb on the farm in Ohio, was having instability problems and had recently fallen three times. I then decided to go up to Ohio with the primary focus of being with her and helping to be there through whatever the future held. I knew that this would be a major diversion for me, but I felt that this is what the Lord would honor, and Katie would be pleased. In early June, I joined Barb on the farm and stayed for about two weeks while her stability seemed to be much better.

I then decided to put the boat into the marina again in Cheboygan for two weeks, beginning in mid-June. I went north to the cottage at Douglas Lake where the boat was stored, to prepare it launching. When I arrived, the weather was rainy, very cool, and not pleasant to be on the water. As a result, I just lived on the boat for the entire two weeks. Power was available from the cottage, as well as the other amenities. I then proceeded to spend the entire two weeks cleaning the inside, re-painting, repairing, and oiling the teak. This kept me very busy and productive. The last few days of the two weeks, the weather turned nice, so I then proceeded to clean and polish the outside hull. This completed a face-lift that was badly needed after thirty-nine years of use. I then covered it completely, prepared *Empathy* for winter storage, and proceeded back to the farm to be with Barb.

The amazing thing about this two-week hibernation in the boat, not one moment of this time was I lonely. I had purchased a wonderful portable speaker that, along with my iPhone, played my favorite easy-listening songs of the '40s and '50s. Also, I had a friend, Gail from our Bible study group, who I communicated with every few days to "do life" together, just as friends. The boat got much needed attention, I was relieved of my loneliness, I felt good about my circumstances, and Gail was helped as well as she had been struggling with depression. Amazing, Lord, how you can help accomplish so much, even during a stormy, rainy period!

In addition, Neil's twin grandsons, Tom and Todd who were twenty-one years old at the time, were living in the cottage where the boat was stored. I was able to get to know these boys much better. They had been raised by Neil and his wife from infancy. One Friday evening, I went into the cottage and they had several of their friends there just having a good time talking. They all welcomed me, and I was amazed that there was no drinking, no smoking—they were all very polite—with no rough language, and no TV. They took me on as Uncle Dean, and I decided that the Lord had me in their lives to befriend and encourage them. I had found out that the State of Michigan had offices in various cities that provided free counseling and awareness of the job opportunities. They informed me that, at that time, there were some twenty-two thousand openings through-out the state that they were aware of. I gathered brochures and infor-mation that I made available to these young people. I felt that I was planting seeds and reflecting the Lord's love through me to these young people, as part of his reason why he had me there.

Meanwhile, back at the farm, Barb was doing okay and I stayed there most of the time until November. I would take numerous breaks to visit my kids and families in Colorado, Connecticut, and Tampa, always returning to the farm in between trips. I also returned to Tampa when a hurricane was approaching, but then returned to Ohio after the event was over. By November, Barb, who was celebrat-ing her ninety-first birthday the next January, said that she felt much better and suggested that I go back to Tampa for Thanksgiving, and she felt able to be alone again.

After settling in back at Tampa, in January of this year, 2018, I became inspired to begin working on this book again. It had been put on hold for the past three years due to all the events causing my life to be in a continual state of transition. At that time, I had expected to have four chapters yet to complete in order to bring my walk up to date, but how do I complete the last chapter? In order to proceed further, I realized that I needed Katie's daily journal that she kept up with throughout our many adventures. I desperately needed her comments to proceed but could not find these journals at home in Tampa. Late in January, I decided that I had apparently left them at the farm and decided to go up for a quick long-weekend visit. I arrived on a Thursday and, as the Lord had orchestrated, the next day was Barb's ninety-first birthday. How special that I was there for the celebration with her kids, Jeff and Sally. I could not find a trace of Katie's notes at the farm, however, and concluded that they had to be somewhere at home in Tampa. At least, Lord, you gave me a reason to be at Barb's birthday! There was, of course, no way for me to know that two weeks later the Lord suddenly took Barb home with him, in her sleep—no struggle, no pain—the same as he took her sister, Katie, to heaven 2 ½ years before.

Ironically, over twenty years before, Barb's husband, Cal, had been suffering for about eight years with Parkinson's disease and dementia. I had a reason to go up on business in the area, so made a short visit to the farm. At the time of my visit, Cal had been unable to communicate thoughts. When I was ready to leave, I gave him a hug and said, "I love you, Cal."

He then replied, "I love you too, Dean."

Amazing! Less than a month later, the Lord took Cal home. The Lord's consistence in doing the unexpected in the last days of my loved ones is so very impacting. Thank you, Holy Spirit, for such a touching way to show your involvement as our end of life approaches.

Late last year, 2017, in my devotion and prayer time with the Lord, he put on my heart the desire to explore the Holy Spirit in detail from life's day-to-day experiences. All of us committed Christians know the Father, the Son Jesus, but what is the Holy Spirit as it is experienced in real time? We know that it is part of the Trinity, but it is hard for us to get our arms around as to how to experience it. Those of us who are students of the Bible know much about the theology, but what about the real-life experiences? We attribute much of our unexplained events in our lives to the Lord—we often give out the expression "Thank you, Lord"—but, to what part of the Trinity does that really refer to? When we ask Jesus into our lives and we are "born again," many of us then experience changes in our lives that are unexplained. In my case, I had a thirst for reading the Bible, where I found an unbelievable amount of wisdom that applied directly to my life. What is this newly developed desire to help others in need—compassion, empathy? It was not explainable to me for all these years, so I just attributed it to "the Lord." How is it that, in our church services or in our Bible study materials, the Holy Spirit is rarely addressed in a way that we can fully understand, and embrace it in our daily lives? How did I come to realize how my life, as described throughout this book, was impacted by my spiritual relationship with God? As I am now writing this book, six months ago I was inspired to explore what I am experiencing with the unseen world around us, and I am blown away with what I am discovering. In my Bible study group, I offered to moderate a discussion on the unseen world that we live in, focusing on the Holy Spirit. As a result of what was uncovered during this discussion, it has opened a major new development in my walk with the Lord. What is currently underway in me is an entirely greater personal relationship with God through the Holy Spirit. I am learning to experience him every day in every way. I am thrilled with this discovery, and he has helped me immensely in my recall of these events and to be inspired to describe them.

The Spirit Song

O let the son of God enfold you—with his Spirit
    and his love.
Let him fill your heart and satisfy your soul.
Oh, let him have the things that hold you—and
    his Spirit, like a dove,
Will descend upon your life and make you whole.

Jesus, O Jesus, come and feed your lambs,
Jesus, O Jesus, come and feed your lambs.

Come and sing this song with gladness, as your
    hearts are filled with joy.
Lift your hands in sweet surrender to his name.
Give him all your tears and sadness, give him all
    your years of pain,
And you'll enter into life in Jesus' name.

—John Wimber

As I began this summer, 2018, I have come to realize that, because of the difficulty of finding seats available as a non-revenue passenger on Southwest flights, I am here for the summer without returning to Tampa. My nephew and his wife, Jeff and Sally, have welcomed me warmly in every way, and I am living by myself in Barb's home. I have come with three goals in mind:

1. to complete the first draft of this book, ready for proofreading;

2. to develop a closer walk with our Lord, through the Holy Spirit; and

3. resolve the residual loneliness from not having Katie in my life.

In regard to my loneliness, I have often mentioned to others that I am presenting an interesting challenge to the Lord—how can he fill the hole in my heart from her loss? Amazingly, I have discovered that he is filling this void, as always, in a way that I would have never expected. When I am not concentrating on my devotions or on composing this book, I always have music playing through a portable speaker system. From the music channel, I select "Easy Listening" that plays the greatest of songs from the '40s and '50s—the Big Band era. These were the songs that Katie and I enjoyed listening to, singing and dancing throughout our lives together. In the past, as I have been playing them, they, of course, would bring back wonderful memories along with a great deal of loneliness. As I came to the farm this summer, the Lord inspired me to turn each love song into a love song to him. I have, and what a difference this has made. This has helped me to neatly resolve my loneliness. As I have mentioned, "Have I Told You Lately That I Love You?" (Lord) Another example is:

> You make me feel so young,
> You make me feel like spring has sprung.
> You make me feel there are songs to be sung.
> And even when I am old and gray
> I'm gonna feel the way that I do today
> 'cause you make me feel so young.

> —Composer—Josef Myrow
> Lyrics by Mack Gordon

As the day came that I was preparing to address this last chapter of this book, I was led by the Spirit to scripture that has, at last, defined why the Lord took my dear Katie to him. As a glimpse of his desire for my remaining days, he brought me to 1 Corinthians 7:32–35:

> I would like you to be free of concern. An unmarried man is concerned about the Lord's affairs—how he can please the Lord. But a married man is concerned about the affairs of this world—how he can please his wife—and his interests are divided…I am saying this for your own good, not to restrict you, but that you may live in a right way in undivided devotion to the Lord.

Finally, this scripture has been revealed to me after three years that I have been without Katie. During this time, I have grown greatly in better understanding what the Lord has already done in guiding, protecting, encouraging, inspiring me, and being disciplined along the way. I have no concept of what he is about to do with me, and I don't need to know. Psalm 139 verse 16 says, "All the days ordained for me were written in Your book before one of them came to be."

Amazingly, this scripture from 1 Corinthians was revealed to me the morning that I was about to address this last chapter of my book—the very day! This illustrates to me the verse in Psalm 139 that says, "…before a word is on my tongue you know it, O Lord." and "How precious are your thoughts, O God! How vast is the sum of them! Were I to count them, they would outnumber the grains of sand."

I conclude this book with an appeal to the Lord from the end of Psalm 139, and I strongly encourage that this also be your appeal: "Search me, O God, and know my heart; test me and know my anxious thoughts. See if there is any offensive way in me, And lead me in the way everlasting."

So, the rest of my life will be with undivided devotion to the Lord, and I consider that my work is never done until he takes me home.

> I am weak but Thou art strong
> Jesus keep me from all wrong

I'll be satisfied as long
As I walk, let me walk close to Thee

Just a closer walk with Thee
Grant it, Jesus, is my plea
Daily walking close to Thee
Let it be, dear Lord, let it be.

When my feeble life is o'er
Time for me will be no more,
Guide me gently, safety o'er
To Thy kingdom's shore, to Thy shore.

—Patsy Cline

(As a final treat, Google "Just a Closer Walk
Thee" and listen to Patsy Cline and Willie Nelson
sing.)

Just remember, if you are "touched" by this message, that special feeling is a spiritual event directly from his Holy Spirit that resides in your life 24-7.

This book is intended to be an appeal to those who read it, to be inspired to seek your own closer walk with the Lord. All it takes is for you to profess a belief in Jesus Christ and you too will be forever accepted into God's heaven. He will then take you, if you are willing and seek him, to take you one step at a time to a better life. However, he doesn't do this to just be a "nice guy"; he has a job for you to do. He has a unique plan for each and every one of us, to go out into our hurting world and live a life that pleases him. And then he wants you to also tell your story to whomever he puts in your life, about what he is doing and has done with your life. He is calling you to help spread his word. You don't have to be special, to be famous, to be successful, to be young, to be educated, to memorize scripture, to preach or to recite scripture, to "clean up your act," or to just be active in your church. He only asks you to be yourself, to "blossom where your planted," and be willing to let him do his work in and through you. Radiate his love in you, serve him faithfully as he leads you, and "Let your light so shine that others may see your good works, and glorify our Father that is in Heaven." The real question is, "Will you follow if He calls you by name?"

The Summons

Will you come and follow me if I but call your
name?
Will you go where you don't know and never be
the same?
Will you let My love be shown, will you let My
name be known,
Will you let My life be grown in You and You
in me?

Will you love the "you" you hide if I but call your
name?
Will you quell the fear inside and never be the same?
Will you use the faith you've found to reshape the
world around,
Through my sight and touch and sound in you
and you in me?

Let me turn and follow You and never be the same.
In Your company I'll go, where Your love and
footsteps show,
Thus I'll move and live and grow, in You and You
in me.

—John L. Bell

Free Preview

_____

Grandpa's Walk with the Lord is an accumulation of twenty chapters in the author's life, giving tribute to the Lord's involvement in the very details of his experiences. This includes growing up in depression days in a small town in Ohio, enduring the challenge of graduating from West Point, and completing pilot training and then becoming an instructor in the early days of single-engine military jets. He flew out of west Texas all over the U.S. as an instructor and then was assigned to Germany for three years. During this time in Germany, he flew all over Europe during the tense time that the Berlin Wall was being constructed. After leaving the Air Force, he conducted international business with nearly all of the airlines, including projects in Ethiopia, Kenya, South Africa, India, Italy, Finland, as well as all of the U.S. airlines. He and his family became sailors starting in the Finger Lakes in New York and then progressing to the Thousand Islands in the St. Lawrence River. Employment took the family to Florida where he still resides thirty-five years later. He has sailed all around Florida and has made five trips to the Bahamas. At age seventy-six, he and his wife then began a two-summer, thrilling journey from Florida up the Intracoastal Waterway all the way to Upper Michigan. Of course, such adventures are accompanied by risks, and that is where he describes the Lord's involvement along the way. The author believes that when we are outside of our comfort zone, that is where we can experience the Lord showing himself in the details.

Keynote: An inspired collection of testimonies where the Lord has been evident in the details of his life.

Meeting Dean, I was blessed to know a man who has shown a deep love of God and a strong faith that just gives off the feeling that his present mission in life is to pass these blessings on. Reading his life story helped me to know how the Lord and the Holy Spirit became such a deep part of him. He is a man who feels blessed and wants others to have it too. Thank you, Dean, for your friendship and for the many people you have touched with your life and your care.

—Gail Fearn

Thank you for asking me to be a part of this book journey. It has helped me to be more aware of the Lord's presence in my life past, present, and in the future.

—Debbie Dow

This book is an intriguing story about the spiritual journey the author has witnessed and continues to walk every day. The author's humility, compassion, and honesty make it easy for the reader to relate and reflect upon. Against all odds, the author survived and as a result becomes stronger and more faithful in his beliefs. His life is a testimony, offering hope, encouragement, and assurance about this life and the next. *Grandpa's Walk with the Lord* not only exercises the body but the mind and soul as well.

—Jennifer McMahon

About the Author

_____

Dean Bates has been an adventurer his entire life including being an Air Force pilot and instructor, international business man, camping, and extensive sailing including five trips to the Bahamas. He graduated from West Point, lived in Germany for three years, and has traveled all over the U.S, Europe, Africa, and elsewhere. His Christian lineage includes the Pilgrims on the Mayflower, Quakers, and pioneer families founding their own churches. He has helped people for over twenty-five years through his own care ministry, including house painting and home repairs for over nineteen years. He is a piano player with a music ministry of his own. In his latter season of life, he feels inspired to tell his story in a way that others may relate and also be inspired.

CPSIA information can be obtained
at www.ICGtesting.com
Printed in the USA
FFHW020117071119
55998456-61848FF